BUTTERF

A Metamorphosis From Death and Destruction Into Life and Liberty

PASTOR JOHN MACINNES

AMBASSADOR INTERNATIONAL
GREENVILLE, SOUTH CAROLINA & BELFAST, NORTHERN IRELAND

www.ambassador-international.com

Butterfly Man
A Metamorphosis from Death and Destruction to Life and Liberty

The Life Story of Pastor John MacInnes

Paperback: ISBN: 978-1-64960-188-9

Printed in UK

Scriptures taken from the KING JAMES VERSION (KJV):

Ambassador International
Emerald House
411 University Ridge, Suite B14
Greenville, SC 29601
www.ambassador-international.com

Ambassador Books and Media
The Mount
2 Woodstock Link
Belfast, BT6 8DD, Northern Ireland, UK
www.ambassadormedia.co.uk

Contents

This is the story of John MacInnes. May God bless this story to all our hearts and may someone be encouraged to do what John MacInnes has been inspired to do. I commend this book to you. It is an amazing testimony of the power of God who has set free a young man from the power of sin. It is true, *"whom the son sets free, he is free indeed"*.

Pastor James McConnell
Late Pastor, Whitewell Metropolitan Tabernacle, Belfast

I first came to know John MacInnes when he came as a student to the Bible College of Wales. During our time together, some details of John's life were shared, but I have found it exciting to read his autobiography which fills in a lot more of the details. I am very happy to recommend this book; it demonstrates the power of God to radically transform a life. Read it and be blessed.

Rev. Dr Colin Hurt
Principal-emeritus, Bible College of Wales, Swansea

I am honoured to be invited to commend this precious book by Pastor John MacInnes, whom I have known for many years. I commend it because it teaches the two most important lessons of all: to be sorry for our past sins and to believe in Jesus Christ as our own personal Saviour. This welcome book of Pastor John illustrates God's words in Metrical Psalm 25, which so many of us sing regularly in church:

My sins and faults of youth Do thou, O Lord, forget:
After thy mercy think on me And for thy goodness great.

Rev. Maurice Roberts
Minister in the Free Church of Scotland (Continuing)
Past Editor of the Banner of Truth Magazine

Foreword

THE FIRST TIME I met John MacInnes I had a strong sense that here was a young man whom God's hand was upon. Over the past years I have seen this young man develop into a vessel that God is using. Not only does John have an amazing testimony, but he lives a godly life. I am so proud to know him personally and have the privilege of encouraging him.

I believe in the future God will use him mightily and anoint him and make him a blessing. You will hear of John MacInnes and the work that God is doing through him in the days that lie ahead.

I commend this book to you. It is an amazing testimony of the power of God who has set free a young man from the power of sin. It is true, *"whom the son sets free, he is free indeed"*.

This is the story of John MacInnes. May God bless this story to all our hearts and may someone be encouraged to do what John MacInnes has been inspired to do.

Pastor James McConnell

Preface

REASONS FOR WRITING THIS BOOK

'WHY AM I WRITING this book?', you may ask. Well, I have mused over that same question as I sit here with no experience of having written one ever before!

I guess one of the many reasons is because Christians have always been writers. The Bible is full of testimonies from individuals through the various ages of how they met with God and how He moved in their lives. They had enormously different backgrounds, levels of education and life experiences. Notwithstanding this, the Bible has a common thread throughout. The central message is the good news of the gospel and how it affects our daily living and, more importantly, our eternal destiny. Man has been given the ability to communicate using the written word and the understanding to read it.

God, Himself wrote the Ten Commandments on tablets of stone (Exodus 20), as well as the writing on the wall at Belshazzar's feast (Daniel 5). I count it a great privilege to now pen my own life story and tell how the Lord has moved in it. This book will mention places I have been, people I have met, with their highs and lows. And then how, when my life seemed all but over, Christ came to me as in the parable of the lost sheep. He found me and carried me to safety in His loving arms (Matthew 18v10-14).

I have endeavoured to be as honest as possible as I have written this book, and yet be sensitive to others from my past. I trust you can appreciate that. It is written with the purpose of healing and building bridges. My principal goal, of course, is to point you to the Lord Jesus Christ who made this great statement in John 14v6: *"Jesus saith unto him, I am the way, the truth, and the life: no man cometh unto the Father, but by me"* I tried many ways – only to hit many a dead end!

I am grateful and humbled to share with you my story which is His story of a passage from bondage to liberty in and through Christ. The central character and hero of this book must be the Lord Jesus Christ Himself. He says: *"I, if I be lifted up from the earth, will draw all men unto me"* (John 12v32). That I shall endeavour to do.

Pastor John MacInnes

CHAPTER 1
METAMORPHOSIS

I WEPT as I considered it. My life had spiralled out of all control over the previous months. My two closest friends snatched from me under tragic circumstances; a broken relationship and having to deal with and all the fallout that creates. My own life in real and imminent danger on several fronts and now, to top it all, here I was lying in a special hospital bed which had been brought in and set up in my own home. I was unable even to shower or dress without assistance. Both my legs were in a plaster cast tied up at the end of the bed with over a thousand stitches in them. There was just my dog and me now, and I could not even take him for a walk! For sure life as I knew it was over! At each stage, I was sure I had bottomed out. Nothing else could surely go wrong, could it?

Many regrets and not a thing I could do about it. Weakness and depression seemed my lot from this day forward. Who would have thought it? Certainly not me. Such a short time ago I seemed to be riding on the crest of a wave. That wave had now crashed against the jagged rocks of life and a damaged broken man was swept up gasping for a breath. Struggling to make any sense of it, and struggling to survive.

Metamorphosis. It's a strange word but what does it mean? Well, it's a Greek word for "transformation." Often used to describe the mutation in the life-cycle of a butterfly, but in many ways remarkably like my own life's journey. Caterpillar to butterfly. It's a fascinating journey to behold with all its different stages:

The egg. Here is an interesting fact: An adult butterfly lays about 400 eggs at a time, although only 8 generally survive. That means 98% never make it to adult life but the 2% that somehow survive demonstrate the miracle and design of creation. Each egg is so tiny and unimpressive, about the size of a pin head. Everyone has only a slim chance of even getting to the point of birth, let alone anything else. Against all the odds, a tiny creature eventually emerges! New beginnings, yet so little potential it would seem. It appears less than mediocre when you see and consider it.

Next, *the larva* or young caterpillar with its limited world vision.

Although they can have six sets of eyes their vision is very poor. They see nothing of the world beyond their immediate circumstances. They have legs attached to their bodies too. Some are load-bearing yet others are false legs and are incapable of supporting them. They destroy everything in their path while growing bigger and bolder all the time. A newborn caterpillar eats its own leaf first before it travels. It is unaware and seemingly unconcerned that it is sabotaging its own territory. The larva is not an attractive creature by any manner of means and it appears to have no hope of any improvement. It seems little more than an eating machine! It does, however, shed its skin as it outgrows it. It casts off that which was soft and supple and develops a new harder exterior. It truly seems to be a creature of its environment. Its destiny seems obvious to all: to eat or be eaten!

Later, the pupa or chrysalis in *its cocoon* seems bound and dying yet even in that place a hidden change is taking place on every level. At this point, it sheds its skin for the last time. They often hang upside down as the process begins and their true colour only is seen at the very final stages of their alteration. Cell and hormone change and even its very DNA is restructured! No one can see nor understand what is going on in there.

This is much like human life, is it not? Many an unfriendly face, or one etched with tiredness or pain, passes us by on the street. But what is going on under the surface? That is the question! A worried mother, or a hurting soul whose life has been broken with disappointment and regrets? One who has lost a loved one and is struggling to cope? The truth is we just never know! This I can tell you, though. Although there are many different problems we all face, we all have a common problem. It is our broken relationship with God. Thankfully, God's own Son came to give us a remedy where there appeared to be none.

Now, I shall certainly not insult your intelligence and tell you that when you become a Christian all problems disappear, for that is not the case. What I can say as comfort is this: you will never have to face them alone. I know what it feels like sitting in a big empty house all alone. I also know what it feels like to be in a room full of people yet it only enforces the disconnect, the facade that your life has become. You laugh on the outside while crying within. To anyone looking in on your world, you seem to have all the trappings and trimmings of success. Yet there is a deep pain, an acknowledgement that all is not well. A desire for happiness that seems so elusive and impossible to grasp hold of from where you find yourself to be.

Christ makes us so many promises in His word such as

Hebrews 13v5: *"for he hath said, I will never leave thee, nor forsake thee."* Or, Proverbs 18v24: *"there is a friend that sticketh closer than a brother."* Trials and difficulties will come as they must. For all that, there is an awareness of His presence. At the toughest times, it can seem most evident and sweet.

Loneliness, as I recall, can seem an awful thing, especially if you are aware you do not like the person you have become. You look in the mirror and see a guy you no longer recognise, nor do you like what you see. He is selfish and hard-hearted.

Yet you are in deep now. It's like being in a deep hole with no way out. Nothing short of a miracle is of any use to you now, but how could that happen?

(4) Finally, you have *the adult butterfly*. It bears no resemblance in any way to how it started. You could scarcely believe it was in any way a relative to the unsightly little larva or caterpillar, let alone the very same species! It now has huge eyes that sense light and images. Other senses are now developing too. It can smell and taste. Its diet is no longer its own skin or its own living environment. It now feeds on nectar and water.

God's word tells us of the experience of being born again, born from above. The Bible puts it in these terms: "*Therefore if any man be in Christ, he is a new creature: old things are passed away; behold, all things are become new*" (2 Corinthians 5v17). That is the experience. I know first-hand. The old has gone and the new has come.

Our butterfly is a colourful, magnificent creature. It has freedom hitherto unknown to it. It has a view of the world from above. It searches for a mate to reproduce. Reproduction is now a primary objective. The Bible teaches us this: "*and the things that thou hast heard of me among many witnesses, the same commit thou to faithful men, who shall be able to teach others also*" (2 Timothy 2v2). In other words, the objective of a true Christian is to share the story of what Christ has done in their lives. Yet more than that, it is with the intention to reproduce. For others to learn, for others to share. The idea behind this verse in the original language is to produce others of the same quality. I hope that in the sharing of my story, you will learn from it. Most importantly, that you will meet the Master of the storms, the Lord Jesus. That you will have your encounter with God and you too in time will share your story. That the cycle of life will spread out as the gospel is shared and affects hearts and lives.

Like our butterfly and my personal experience, I pray that each person reading this book will be "free to fly." Be assured of this: when God does a work in a person's life it is deep and thorough work – a transformation without a doubt. Like the lifecycle of a butterfly, it has many twists and turns. Magical to behold, better to experience. The place real transformation takes place is at the cross of the Lord Jesus Christ.

Of course, this experience is by no means exclusive to me. The Bible is full of characters who have met with God and been inextricably changed. In the Old Testament, there are such people as:

Jacob – a wily man, a cheat and a liar. He met with God and became the Father of a nation, a prince with God.

Moses – a Prince in Egypt. Trained in all its wisdom and ways. The super power of its day. He spent 40 years in the wilderness and emerged as the meekest man on all the earth (Numbers 12v3). He became a great prophet and leader of God's people. Who would have thought it!

The New Testament also has characters such as:

The woman at the well (John 4v1-26). She had so many broken relationships and a broken life to boot. Christ offered her *"living water"* with the promise she would never thirst again. She left her water pot that day with a message of hope and change. *"Come see a man that told me all things that ever I did, is not this the Christ?"* (v39-42).

What of the little 'dislikeable' thief *Zacchaeus*? Greedy, ambitious, unscrupulous and hated! Christ called Him down from his perch by name. By the end of that day, salvation had come to His house. It is like the story of Scrooge – but it's no fairy tale! He went from a sinner to a son just as quick as that!

The Apostle *Paul* – a self-righteous Pharisee (Philippians 3v1-11; Acts 26v12-17). 'Hell-bent' on wreaking havoc among

Christians. "*...breathing out threatening and slaughter*" (Acts 8v13; 9v1-2). He was met by the risen Christ on the Damascus Road. He asked a great question that day "*who are you, Lord?*" He got the same answer you will get if you ask with sincerity of heart: "*I am Jesus.*" The chief persecutor became a chief apostle!

Finally, consider *the thief on the cross* (Luke 23v39-43). His life was all but over. Too late for good works; too late to go to church. All he could do was look to Christ and cry out for mercy. I dare say most of us would think he got what he deserved. But hear him cry out: "*Remember me when you come into your kingdom.*" Others saw a man dying in agony on that central cross. This man saw a King with a Kingdom, with power to take even the lowest and most lost with Him there! Some saw a defeated upstart, but he saw a victor, a conqueror and a Saviour.

What do you see as you look at the cross, my friend? A man dying that does not affect you? Or do you see with the eyes of faith? Can you see your great need and can you see a great Saviour? Both thieves were within touching distance of Christ. They were that close that day. One went out into eternity without Him, a lost soul.

The other found the life and forgiveness of Christ. His day started badly, but it ended well. For Jesus heard his plea and gave him this great promise: "*today you shall be with me in paradise.*"

That, my dear friend, is the One I want to introduce you to in the course of reading this book. Yes, it is my story, as each of the Bible characters mentioned had theirs. But what of you today as you read these words – what is your story? Can you identify with any of these people? Are your broken, self-righteousness, far from God or just plain lost? You may indeed feel you are far away from God. Yet the truth is this.

You are only one true heart's-cry away from God moving in your life. James wrote: *"Draw near to God, and He will draw near to you"* (James 4v8).

I pray God's Holy Spirit will quicken and awaken you as you read this book. It is only He who can make you aware of your great need. It is only He who can bring you God's life. It is only He that can produce real change. Not some superficial skin-deep change, but a change from the inside out as you are born again just as Jesus taught (John 3v5, 7).

Chapter 2

THE EGG HATCHES

A BABY BOY is born. John Angus MacInnes 8lb 4oz, first born son of Iain and Margaret MacInnes in Kilmarnock Royal Infirmary 10th of July 1968. My parents had married just a year before. My dad was 24 and my mum 21.

My father was then a butcher who would later go on to work for himself. First as a grocer then later as a car salesman and second-hand furniture dealer. His background was a troubled one. His parents had split while he was young and his dad who had been a policeman had died of a heart attack at only fifty years of age. Dad got into some scrapes while growing up.

In this 1918 photo taken at Crookedholm, near Kilmarnock, great-grandfather John Gorrie is on the left with his brother Robert in the middle and their father, Andrew, on the right.

My grandfather came to faith in Christ in his later years. I recently found an old book of his, which I found most helpful, by the famous old Scottish preacher, Robert Murray M'Cheyne (1813-1843), as I was preparing for a sermon. God's plans and purposes are truly amazing. Whoever could have conceived that a book purchased long before I was even thought of in this world would one day help to mould a preacher!

Back to my dad. It does appear meeting my mum seemed to have been a calming influence in his life at least in part for a time. My mum was always ambitious and business-minded. Her grandparents had owned a small grocer's shop and the knowledge she had gained would prove invaluable as they ventured out on their own. She would later deal in the second hand and antique business till her retirement. Her mother had died of cancer at only forty-two years of age, just after I was born. This was a seismic event in her life both as a young newlywed and mother. Still, she has always been a strong character with a desire to bring us up in the best way possible, and equip us for life. I have never doubted her love or devotion to us.

Two years later almost to the day (14th July) my twin sisters, Margaret and Christine, were born. Fourteen years later Joanna would come along as a late baby too.

The shop was in a particularly rough part of our town. So rough it was demolished and the people relocated to other areas! That said it was a very successful small business, netting in around £1000 profit per week over fifty years ago.

My mum who was always our rock and was looking out for the best for us was concerned and she did not want us brought up in a tough environment. I can remember the shop having iron bars on the window and several guard dogs! I thought nothing of it at the time of course as I was blissfully unaware of our surroundings. My parents decided to sell up and move to a neighbouring village where mum had been born - Hurlford, a place I would live throughout my teenage years.

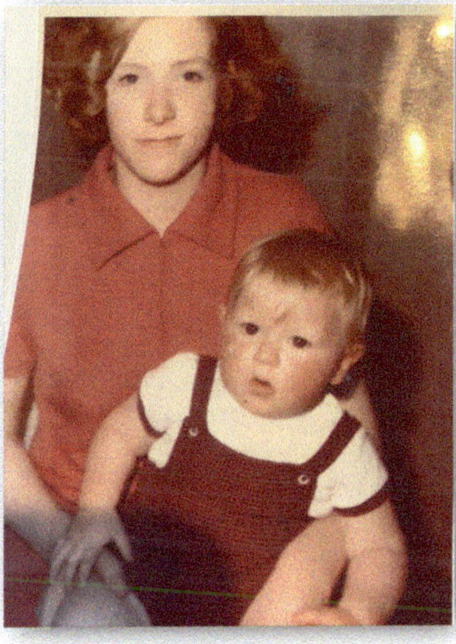

On mum's knee

It showed great sacrifice and love for us to move in an attempt to keep us all on the right track. Now here is the problem, and in ministry, I have seen it often. The human problem is not primarily a problem of the social environment, neither is it first and foremost an education issue.

Our first parents, Adam and Eve, were in the perfect environment (Genesis 1-2). No social issues, no neighbour disputes, perfect working conditions with no financial strain. Guess what? They still had problems! They came from within, from their hearts and desires (Genesis 3).

That is our biggest problem: ourselves! The sin problem. We have a natural inclination to do what is wrong or sinful as the Bible calls it (Romans 3v23; 5v12). I believe that is easy to observe. You do not need to teach a child how to tell a lie. Put them under pressure and that thought will come to them. You teach them to always tell the truth. Neither do you teach them to say unkind words. Listen to children argue, at times they can be very cruel. Kindness is what must be taught.

So, unfortunately, it would turn out that in later life I would have a natural inclination also for that which was wrong. I chose a lifestyle that would cause hurt to others and myself. Much later I would find out that the change required is a change of heart. The Old Testament Prophet Ezekiel puts it like this:

> *'A new heart also will I give you, and a new spirit will I put within you: and I will take away the stony heart out of your flesh, and I will give you an heart of flesh. And I will put my spirit within you, and cause you to walk in my statutes, and ye shall keep my judgments, and do them.'* (Ezekiel 36v26-27)

A heart transplant operation by God the Creator. The Great Physician Jesus Christ is the only one capable of such a delicate operation to be sure.

We were well feed and cared for. Our home was a typical Scottish family environment. God was not mentioned at all as far as I remember, though we were sent to the local Sunday School. Mum would give us money for the collection. I put half in (sometimes) and went to the local café to buy sweets with the rest!

With Grandpa Gorrie (c1970)

Of course, in those days school started or ended with the Lord's Prayer. I remember being taught that in Primary One at Hurlford Primary School. It had no real meaning to me and was repeated by rote just before the free bottle of milk was given out.

Now, here is a thing, for we are told in Isaiah that God's word does not return empty but it accomplishes what is intended for it (55v11). My advice for any parent is to sow God's word into your children at the very earliest opportunity and continue to do so throughout their lives. Why? That word changes lives! That word is power! That word is God-breathed! Even if you see little or no obvious benefit whatsoever. It can take years to come to fruition yet the seed is sown.

With Granny Gorrie (c1983)

At lunch time I would walk to my great gran and grandpa's house. It was only a few minutes from my school. I loved them both dearly. Gran Gorrie would make me such treats as chips and beetroot with either custard to follow, or rice with a dollop of strawberry jam for pudding. There was always chocolate from the top drawer to follow.

My mum and dad loved me. I knew that of course. They were always so busy working to improve our lives. My old grandpa (Gorrie) had retired years before I was around. I can remember cuddling up to him. Telling me stories and singing as I would fall asleep on his well-padded and comfy stomach. He generally wore a warm woollen brown front buttoning cardigan and he smelt of mints. I would slip my tiny hand into the pocket of his cardigan as I lay there and always find a polo mint or a Murray mint for myself. He knew very well exactly what I was doing but never let on he was aware of it. I felt safe and happy. He would teach us little nursery rhymes and things of that nature.

I recall one day having a bit of trouble with a boy at school. He showed me how to make a fist – 'a bunch of fives'. Handy, I thought; I must remember that. In future years there were many occasions I would form that same fist.

I cast my mind back to coming in at lunch one day but on this occasion, the atmosphere was quite different. I had never known anything quite like it. It was tense and heavy, yet I was only seven years old and had no real clue what was going on. My grandpa was in bed, he did not look well, I could see that. They called me in and he stroked my hair. He gave me a five pence coin to go to the shops for some sweets. You could get a lot for 5p then! A bag of crisps was only 2p. I never spent it, though, and kept it safe for years.

Well, I never did see him again. He passed away. I remember my great-gran crying and all the family round about. They had been married over sixty happy years.

That was the first taste of death I would experience. It was so sad. Confusing for a child to try and grasp. What did they mean that he was gone? Where? Why could he not come back? Yet somewhere deep inside I knew it to be true. There was a sense of bewilderment, loss, pain and even anger. It just seemed so unfair. It was the shock and finality of it all that hit home. I would again feel these same sensations many times as I became an adult. You learn to mask it better of course. It changes not a thing for the pain and questions are always there.

So many times, people have come to me as a Pastor in great anguish and distress. Some have relationship issues, others health problems and yet others are suffering from grief. It is an amazing thing how God can use even the brokenness of our past lives to help others who are going through similar experiences. Empathy is a quality that best comes from experience and not a textbook.

I think a lot of people imagine those involved in church ministry came down with the last shower of rain and zero life experience. I can assure you that has not been my own experience. For good or for bad our past shapes us. Yet only

Jesus Christ can remake us! He is the One who could say in John 14v27: *"Peace I leave with you, my peace I give unto you: not as the world giveth, give I unto you. Let not your heart be troubled, neither let it be afraid."* Or in Luke 7: *"And when the Lord saw her, he had compassion on her, and said unto her, Weep not"* (v13). It is Christ who conquers our fears and sorrows. It is He who brings gladness and joy.

So, there begins the life of young John. Full of paradoxes from the very start. Potential, as with all young kids, yet also the early signs of a life journey that would be fraught with difficulties.

Chapter 3

BIG CHANGES AT HOME

I SETTLED into my new school. It and all seemed fine to me as I recall. These were different times back then and I remember being given two of the belt when I was 7. I recollect what it was like to be called to the front of the class and the sting in my hands. I remember the teacher's name and thought, "I owe you one. Some day I will pay you back for that!" Unfortunately, that was an attitude I carried around with me for many years of my life. Holding grudges is neither a good nor a godly thing. Thank God, He is not like that: *"If thou, LORD, shouldest mark iniquities, O Lord, who shall stand? But there is forgiveness with thee, that thou mayest be feared"* (Psalm 130v3-4). *Human* nature tends to hold grudges and keep accounts of when we consider we have been wronged. *God's* nature is to forgive all who ask from a sincere heart and approach Him through the sacrifice of His Son.

Age 10 was a big year in my life. My mum who was a morally upright person was going through a massive transformation. She had become a Christian. She had been born again – and that meant a lot of changes at home! Of course, I didn't exactly know what was going on but I did realise it was a big deal!

With my twin sisters

We were taken regularly to church now. It seemed a bit dull to me and over my head but I loved the people and they showed great love for me. I remember my first minister, Mr Roberts (we are still good friends to this day over forty years later). He was kind to me, taught me verses in Bible class. He started up a club called 'The Friday Club' where we had fun and played table tennis. He also taught me how to play chess, a game which I have enjoyed and that has brought me much pleasure throughout the years. I started to play for my school and then my district as a kid. I joined the Kilmarnock chess club and played for them too. Those guys were adults and were good to me. Great memories, and good for the mind too. It taught me to analyse things, to break things down. To spend time thinking alone is something of course that I do a lot today as a minister. God uses things from our past lives you would never imagine. Things that seem unimportant at the time and yet help shape the people we ultimately become.

Our Friday evenings always ended with a short Bible story. I remember a prayer he once taught me to pray: "Lord shew me *myself* and Lord shew me *thyself*." It meant little to me then, yet to this very day, I pray that short prayer on a fairly regular basis.

That, my friend, is where the born-again experience starts for many: A realisation in some sense at any rate of who we are (not a good person, not perfect before God); then a revelation of who God is (holy, just, loving and forgiving). Without Him, we are lost. In Him, we have newness of life.

I started to become more aware all was not well at home. My parents had a strained marriage. My father was prone to drink and not a lot of fun to be around when he did. He loved us without a doubt but one drink would cause his mood to change, a few and you knew trouble was ahead. They were now pulling in very different directions and inevitably something had to give.

The truth is that there was a lot of fighting in the house, both verbal and physical. I found myself often in the middle of it as a young boy. I got quite used to it especially late on a Friday night, pub night. It is not a good thing to get used to violence. There came a day as I got older it would hardly trouble me at all.

I have thought long and hard about whether to include this in my story or whitewash it out. After careful consideration, I believe there may be people reading this who are currently or previously have experienced similar. I want you to know that Christ sometimes takes us out of difficult situations and other times takes us through them. Without a doubt, my experiences in early life shaped the person I became, and if not a liking for violence certainly a familiarity being around it.

Later at school, as I reached age eleven, I became a Prefect. This involved some very limited responsibilities. I have to chuckle sometimes as my mum says from time to time that I could not have been that bad a person as I was a Prefect at school. A mother's love is a wonderful thing and my mum was and still is, always willing to look for the best in me.

Like our young caterpillar, I was starting to develop as my own little individual. I liked my own company and I also enjoyed the older company too. Apart from my wife, Danielle, and my kids I am still much like that. I am happy to spend time on my own and can think of three or four older ministers (some in their seventies and eighties) that I find fascinating characters.

As I touched upon before, never underestimate how important it is to plant good things into a child's life. As the saying goes, you reap what you sow. If a farmer were to sow a field full of carrot seeds you would be astonished if cabbages came up! Likewise, when God's word and ways are sown, good things will start to flourish. There is a time and process between a seed going into the ground and the final product. Sowing can seem such a thankless task, futile even, but it isn't you know!

If you never sow, you never can reap. Likewise, when the wrong things are sown, the wrong things result: *"Be not deceived; God is not mocked: for whatsoever a man soweth, that shall he also reap. For he that soweth to his flesh shall of the flesh reap corruption; but he that soweth to the Spirit shall of the Spirit reap life everlasting"* (Galatians 6v7-8). If you have never done so till now, start sowing today, make it intentional, and look out for the results!

CHAPTER 4

THE TEENAGE YEARS

THE TEENAGE YEARS can be turbulent for anyone one and I was no exception. I went to secondary school Loudon Academy, Galston, East Ayrshire. I quite enjoyed my school years, although I never really applied myself too much. I did for the most part keep out of trouble. Fighting at home made me somewhat adverse to it at school.

My youngest sister Joanna was born when I was fourteen. It was a difficult birth. She was put immediately on a ventilator to help her breathe. The doctors advised my mum to go along and see her as she might not survive.

My mum had such strong faith. She had just read a Bible verse and quoted it: *"Shall I bring to the birth, and not cause to bring forth? saith the LORD: shall I cause to bring forth, and shut the womb? saith thy God"* (Isaiah 66:9). On saying that she peacefully went to sleep. My sister Joanna survived, thrived and has been a missionary in the Philippines for many years.

Shortly after that, we relocated to a new church where my mum seemed to settle in very well. That said, it was further away and had more meetings. As I recall there were now huge tensions in our home. My mum grew in her faith and my father and she drifted even more then.

I liked the church as it had more people of my age. It is strange now to consider how many gospel messages I sat through in my life seemingly unaffected. I did make a profession as a youngster which I really thought was genuine. That is always the danger with 'kirk kids'. They are perhaps not running to the same excesses as many of their peers. It is easy to be blinded by that fact and assume that you must be in right standing with God. In hindsight, I am now aware at that time there was no deep change or hunger for God in my life.

I left school at 17 and started to work in the family businesses. My dad sold cars; my mum antiques. I remember my first wage of £50. I felt like I was loaded! I don't know if business acumen runs in the blood or not, but I do know I soon realised I could turn a pound. I hired out a stall at a local market and sold all sorts of things. Old tools, crockery, jewellery etc. I also bought my first car for £10. I sold it on and bought 'a good one' for £90!

I had a great opportunity to keep selling my cars for a little extra as that was my dad's line of work. He had a special ramp out front where he would park his 'deal of the week' (always one of his best ones) for all to see. I would nip in when he went out and park my old banger there. But I found myself on the receiving end of a well-deserved row several times. Funny when I think about it now.

My chess, however, was now starting to go on the back burner. I had a school teacher, Mr Armour, who encouraged me in it. He was a good player and was very good to me. I liked him a lot. When I returned to play later in life, he said to me one day. "Stop calling me Mr Armour – just call me Jim." I could never bring myself to do it. Now I was in the awkward position of not knowing what to call him!

Like many teenagers, I was skinny as a rake. I decided lifting weights would help fill me out a bit. It did right enough and at one point after many years I had doubled my original body weight! Still, I liked the way my body was developing.

I was more muscular, stronger and with it came a new found confidence. My dad and I would fight as we often had before – now it was much more even.

That vulnerable feeling was passing and a feeling of self-confidence was quickly replacing it now. In Luke' gospel, we read: *"Jesus increased in wisdom and stature, and in favour with God and man"* (2:52). This verse speaks of Jesus as a young man. He grew wiser, physically more mature and in favour with both God and man. I grew physically bigger and more worldly-wise. I gathered new friends around me and God and church were now less important in my life. Moving away from God never ends well for anyone and I was no exception.

My parents eventually broke up, which was no surprise and to be honest probably felt like a bit of a relief. Still, onwards and upwards! Dad eventually remarried and now I am blessed to have two half-brothers and three half-sisters.

I was young and fit and full of enthusiasm. Life, I believed, must be on the up and up! There is a saying that goes: 'You can't put an old head on young shoulders.' Meaning that young people often think they know best yet have little experience and skills for life's great journey.

I love the story of 'The Prodigal Son' in Luke 15:

> *"And he said, A certain man had two sons: And the younger of them said to his father, Father, give me the portion of goods that falleth to me. And he divided unto them his living"* (11-12):

Here was a young guy who knew best. He just needed cash to achieve his dreams. Young men often suffer from that affliction. No one can tell them, and they feel the masters of their destiny. The teenage John was just such a guy.

The old Father in our story knew best of course. Even his critical older brother knew how it would end. If you have never read this story, I do urge you to take time out and read over that chapter. The renowned author, Charles Dickens, who knew more about writing than most, described it like this "It is the finest short story ever written." We will refer to that story from time to time in this book. Hopefully, the similarities will not be lost on you.

All the signs of trouble ahead were now on the horizon. To any young person reading this, I would urge you to heed those signs in your own life. Seek out the council of older, wiser, Christian folks. Better still, find someone you trust who has time and patience to mentor you. Someone who genuinely loves you and is looking out for your best interests. The best advice I can give you is Bible advice. The greatest teacher of it was the Lord Jesus Christ Himself.

CHAPTER 5
DECISIONS AND DIVISIONS

I WAS NOW a bit older and more comfortable in my skin. Believing I was free to do as I please.

Here is the thing. In the garden of Eden, our first parents made a wrong choice with devastating consequences. Since that day we still have had freedom of choice. There was one big problem though. All our choices are made using a fallen sinful nature. We have a propensity for what is not good for us or others and is at logger heads with God. Yes, I was free to do what I wanted. The question is, what was it I wanted to do?

Many areas of my life were about to change dramatically. There were big decisions ahead, and for the most part selfishness and inexperience influenced how they were made. I joined a local gym that had several serious competitive bodybuilders. I was training hard and adding a good bit of muscle now. Yet these guys had a different look. Bigger and harder, these guys seemed to have an edge. I started partnering up with the gym owner who became my very good friend. He was a lot stronger than I was. Of course, he had years of training over me for one thing. He knew a lot about nutrition, an area I would study extensively as the years would go by. Many a time I would sit and weigh out grams of proteins and carbohydrates trying to get it just right.

One day for the first time I heard the 's' word – anabolic steroids! Now I had another decision to weigh up. I read into it and particularly the negative impact on one's health. Yet, so many guys were big and strong and not one of them seemed to have any negative effects. Ok, I was going to do it! Just 200 tablets over 6 weeks. No big deal!

I took them and put on 10 clean pounds of muscle! No way; this was too good to be true! I tried it again, and this time got very little from it. Oral steroids, I would find out, are sore on your internal organs and a lot of the effect is lost as they break down. Injections are the next thing to try. Well, in for a penny in for a pound. I ordered up a course.

Over the years I became a heavy steroid user. I used pharmaceutical-grade ones, veterinary ones, growth hormones and much more. My eating was good now and my training much better. The problem is, this was an expensive old game. I would need to supplement my income somehow.

Bigger and badder

Many of my friends were involved in the supply of steroids. (At the time the law had quite a few grey areas that have since been tightened up). Others worked in nightclubs as door security. A few of my chums worked in a rough night club and I was invited to come on board with them. You had a mixture of guys such as bodybuilders, boxers, martial artists etc. It was at this time I also started to take a very keen interest in martial arts.

Night clubs have a draw no doubt about it. If you pass by often you will see bright lights, well dressed physical guys at the door and pretty girls welcoming you in. I must have worked in scores of them over the years. Yet one thing was similar in each one of them: once inside you are often immediately plunged into darkness. They look so wholesome yet have many a pitfall for the unsuspecting soul.

All of a sudden everything that was off-limits now seems so readily available. Often casual encounters are as easy to find as a beer at the bar. Drugs are often available too. I never thought I would try that yet it would only take a shake-up in my life for that door to open.

My friend Malcolm seemed to be doing very well. He owned the gym, worked the doors, was good looking and well educated, and was a hit with the ladies. We trained together five days a week. We worked in the clubs four nights a week and hung around a lot during the day. He was 29 and I just turned 21. I remember we just finished a workout where we were joking around after it. We arranged to meet that evening to go to work.

Suddenly I received a phone call right out of the blue though that would again rock my world! Someone said he was dead. That could not be right! I knew it must be wrong.

"Who told you that?"

"How can that be?"

"How did it happen?"

A one-word answer was given – suicide. My head swooned and I felt physically sick. It was true though. You never know what is going on in someone's life no matter how well you think you know them.

There is this verse in the book of Proverbs: *"There is a way which seemeth right unto a man, but the end thereof are the ways of death"* (14:12). Turns out yet again the Bible is proved to be right.

Yet, having seen my first casualty of the lifestyle, I was now actively *embracing*, rather than *turning* from it. I now threw myself headlong into it.

I had never been a drinker as fitness was always my goal. Yet around that time many a night, I would roll home drunk. That did not get rid of the pain. Neither did I like the hangovers or the inability to train the next day. No good I thought – I must try and find happiness elsewhere.

It was a few years further on, but I clearly remember the first time I used a recreational drug. I remember the company I was in (a former policeman!). I remember the bar and the time. I thought it through with this line of reasoning: If I don't like it, I will never do it again – simple really! What I failed to factor in, is what would happen if I did like it. And boy, did I like it!

One single ecstasy tablet – it was called a rhubarb and custard. A single capsule half red and half yellow inside was the drug MDMA (easy to get in the circles I was in). I took it and waited to see... Forty-five minutes later – bang! The music was louder and more appealing, the hairs on the back of my neck were standing on end. I looked around at the girls and felt super confident. I could talk to anyone. No fear or anxiety, no pain or depressing thoughts. It felt amazing, with a great feeling of euphoria.

I was at that time unaware that for each high you get, the next day you will encounter an equivalent low. That is one of the reasons people get hooked on drugs. They are chasing the highs and trying to avoid the lows.

If anyone remembers their Physics from school, you were probably made aware of Newton's 3rd Law: "for every action, there is an equal and opposite reaction." Turns out it's true with drugs too!

Over the years I would become a regular drug user. "Uppers" were my thing. Ecstasy, cocaine and speed in particular. Later would come cannabis and "downers," such as valium and temazepam. I had no clue about any of that, though, on that first night.

Church of course now held little interest for me. Here I had made a whole new life for myself. Leaving the 'f' out of life was the truth, for living a lie is not a life. But I was making a name for myself in these circles now. I recall when in church being told if I left all these, bad things would happen to me. Ok, I had experienced one huge setback but generally, life felt good. I put the things of God and eternity to the back of my mind. From now on I would live life to the full in the here and now.

It's here that I feel I should touch on a sensitive subject that is important to mention as this book maps out my life story. I got married when I was just turned 20 years old. My ex-wife is now happily remarried with children, and as you will find out in the reading of this book, I am now too. I feel it would be inappropriate to mention many details as spouses and offspring may feel uncomfortable with them. I have caused enough pain over the years and am loath to cause any more. I can honestly say however that I am truly sorry for all the grief that resulted from my actions.

Enough to say that no one could have been happy around me in those days. My moods fluctuated due to my steroid abuse. Many a night I would soak a blood-covered shirt in cold water and salt after a nightclub altercation. I was carrying a lot of baggage from my past and in retrospect, the marriage had little chance of survival. I accept full responsibility for the breakdown of it. It was yet another self-inflicted injury.

Now the Bible is very clear on the subject of divorce. It is a very serious thing. In fact, in the last book of the Old Testament the book of Malachi, God says He hates divorce. I am however aware perhaps someone reading this may be a divorcee. I do want to make you aware that though it is the end of a human relationship it does not automatically exclude you from being or becoming a true Christian. In John 4, Jesus meets a woman at a well and strikes up a conversation with her. Turns out she was a divorcee who had five previous husbands and was now in a relationship with a man who was not her husband. I tell you right now many in churches would have written her off. Not Jesus though. He drew her in and offered her *"living water."* He then however addressed her immediate situation. He did not skip over it or treat it flippantly. The result, she was born again and mightily used to tell others of Jesus.

You may have things in your past you are ashamed of. (Most families do). I want to assure you Jesus Christ can address them and forgive and use you. The woman had a history no doubt - but Christ was interested in her new beginning.

Here are some instances from the Bible that will give hope for the hopeless:

Rahab in the Old Testament was a prostitute - she changed and is actually in Jesus birth line.

Rachel was ugly and unloved - yet she was a mother in Israel.

Lazarus in the New Testament was dead and stinking. It does not get much worse than that. Jesus raised him and blessed him.

If it can happen for these characters the good news is that it can still happen today for you too.

CHAPTER 6
THE SWEET SMELL OF SUCCESS

I FELT I had sacrificed a lot of time and energy in my pursuit of a new life and success. Amazingly, all of a sudden it seemed to just come good. I had climbed the ladder in the circles I was involved in. Many of my friends were wealthy and well connected. I had been learning to speak a bit of Spanish and now was doing some business with guys who owned nightclubs and strip joints in Spain. Some were involved in pretty high-end criminal activities. The one I knew best got quite a bit of time in jail for stealing and reselling high-end cars such as Ferraris, Porsches, Jaguars, etc.

I now lived in a much better house. I would move quite frequently and property was something that interested me. I realised I could spot one, oversee the renovation of it, and be quid's-in! I was driving a top of the range car myself. My first was a convertible Mercedes. I would jump back and forth between big robust 4-wheel drive jeeps and sports cars like Porsches and Aston Martins. I had learned from my friend that it was far better to work hard for it and get it legally. That way you can keep it and your liberty! I wore a gold Rolex watch that was the price of some people's homes. I had the best of designer clothes and money was no object to me.

I was now travelling all over the world in the line of work I was involved in. Visiting USA, Mexico, Brazil, Columbia, Thailand, Hong Kong, to name but a few of the places. I was often more abroad than I was in the UK. My home town of Kilmarnock is not a fancy place but I knew it well and always gravitated back to it. I genuinely missed it when I was away yet as soon as I arrived at its borders in my car I would often look around and muse over the question "What was I thinking, what is there to miss?"

I became part-owner of a trendy bar in a nearby town and a place I had once been a doorman at was now mine. Things were on the up and up! I felt like the proverbial self-made man. Even in the UK, I was now moving in some pretty heavy circles with some serious backup when required.

I now had the privilege of training with elite martial artists, including a multi-titled world champion on a one-to-one basis in grappling type sports and wrestling, as well as a multi-titled world champion heavyweight Thai boxer. My confidence was now through the roof. I felt like I had it all.

UK body-building champion-ships, many moons ago!

I still managed to have time to compete at a decent level in bodybuilding too. My training partner of many years and good friend, Derek, won the Mr Britain contest and placed 5th in the Mr Universe event that year. Looking back on it, I probably could have achieved a lot more in martial arts and bodybuilding.

Though I trained hard, I also loved the party life. I remember one night I could not be bothered driving, and instead ordered a taxi from Newcastle (which was a regular stomping ground of mine) to Kilmarnock – a trip of 170 miles. I had an easy-come easy-go attitude to life for sure. I went out in a large group of around 20 lads pretty much every week. I was also in a new relationship that seemed to tick all my boxes. Life was so good I almost had to pinch myself to see if this was real. I felt like I was living the dream.

I remembered with some pleasure some of the old fuddyduddies telling me their woeful tales of how this would all end badly. How sheltered and shallow their idea of life. If only they knew, I thought.

The pursuit of ever-increasing wealth is a futile ambition. You never quite have enough to make you truly happy. You buy a bigger house but the thrill soon wears off. A new top-end sports car but six weeks later it's just another car. Move into wealthier circles and you go from the top of the food chain to the bottom again. If you have £10, then £100 seems a lot. If you have £1,000, it's £10,000. If you have £100,000, a million seems the goal, and so on.

Here is a story in Luke's gospel that sums it up better than I ever could:

> *"And he spake a parable unto them, saying, The ground of a certain rich man brought forth plentifully: And he thought within himself, saying, What shall I do, because I have no room where to bestow my fruits? And he said, This will I do: I will pull down my barns, and build greater; and there will I bestow all my fruits and my goods. And I will say to my soul, Soul, thou hast much goods laid up for many years; take thine ease, eat, drink, and be merry. But God said unto him, Thou fool, this night thy soul shall be required of thee: then whose shall those things be, which thou hast provided? So is he that layeth up treasure for himself, and is not rich toward God."* (Luke 12:16-21)

Every time I seemed to achieve a new level, I found some momentary satisfaction. Yet it was fleeting and the chase felt more exhilarating than the achievement. I used to believe with wealth would come happiness. I found it did not but used to jokingly say it does buy you a better class of misery! When you are in the rat race you just want more, bigger, better and newer. Yet the reality is one day we will all face death and it does not matter how much you have earned, your fame or achievements for you just can't take it with you. It's you and God – an explanation of your life will be required. In the passage we quoted in Luke, I dare say many would have thought the rich man a great success. God's verdict was very different "*thou* fool." The word "*thou*", or "you" in modern lingo, is not in the original but is put in to help with the translation and give sense. It's a one-word verdict of a man's whole life and achievements – "fool!"

Imagine living your whole life thinking you are doing well to have it summed up in one word like that! What a shock – and too late to change. It's a better ending in the story of the prodigal son. Though he blew a fortune there was a day we are told "he came to himself" as he realised he was perishing. He finally comprehended that only his Father could help him now.

I pray each person reading this book will have a consciousness of areas that are lacking in their lives as God's Holy Spirit illuminates such areas and points them to the Lord Jesus Christ. Please believe me, dear friend, it does not matter how successful you become or the 'big names' you meet, there is no one like Jesus. It matters not what highs you achieve – there is no high like the Most High God.

CHAPTER 7
FAILING TO TAKE STOCK

ANY SUCCESSFUL business person involved in buying and selling must regularly take stock. Otherwise, one has no clue what is going on. It's all the difference between being a roaring success or bankruptcy.

What was the cost price of an item?

What will it retail for?

How many do I have? Do I need more?

The big question is: At the end of it all, was it worth it?

I was on the ball with this sort of thing. I monitored stock levels, exchange rates and all that was required of a budding young entrepreneur.

Unfortunately, in my personal life, I miserably failed to do so! I did not ask the same important questions:

What is the cost of it all?

What do I have?

Is it all worth it?

A fair price or was the price just far too high?

What do I mean by that, you may ask?

Well, I certainly was capable of causing a lot of pain in other people's lives, albeit at times unintentionally. Relationships and friendships were ripped apart without much consideration of others.

My family must have been under great stress watching my life spiralling out of control. You rarely think of that at the time. The Bible teaches us of the Holy Trinity (Father, Son and Holy Ghost) My life now revolved around an 'unholy trinity', in the lifestyle I so loved and was embroiled in: me, myself and I.

The crowd I was now running with could be very violent at times. The truth is, that on occasion people got hurt. The brutality I had witnessed and been involved in as a nightclub bouncer seemed quite tame now compared with some of the bloodshed that it had now escalated to. I am certainly not proud of the violence in my life. I don't want to sensationalise it or make it look attractive in any way. The harsh reality is that the lifestyle of violence brought only misery to those involved in it. Blood, tears and snotters! Pain, shame and searing of your conscience to boot. You hurt and you get hurt whether you are aware of it or not. Yet, I do not want to whitewash this but I can say I am genuinely sorry for all that came to pass in that era. I feel I must give you at least a flavour of my past before contrasting it with the new life I have found in Christ today.

The goalposts were now ever-shifting. What was unacceptable at one point now became acceptable and even the norm. The role of drugs had also changed again. Steroids were no longer used for an edge. I took them for 6 months of the year and even when 'off', i.e., though not physically taking them they were for the most part still in my system. Recreational drugs, as they are often referred to, were also no longer just for highs. They were now a regular part of my weekly routine. The feelings of euphoria had now been replaced by a sense of getting by. As I climbed the ladder, in one sense I was in free fall ethically, morally and spiritually.

There is a well-known saying that goes like this: "failing to prepare is preparing to fail." That, unfortunately, was where

'Big John', also known by some of my friends as 'Mad dog MacInnes', was now heading!

There is a story in 1 Samuel 25 which I invite you to read at your convenience. Time does not permit us to go into it in great depth, but here are some of the highlights of lowlights of it. To be more precise: The godly King David had shown kindness to a man called Nabal. He asked for very little in return but was rudely turned down most dismissively. David's anger is kindled against this ungrateful miserly man. Nabal is hard-hearted and cynical in the extreme. He is described as "a churlish man" (rude, fierce, ungracious, ungrateful, barbaric, merciless and much more). His old heart was now unyielding as a stone and he died a tragic death embittered to the end. He had so much and lost it all! Never be a Nabal, my friend. Keep short accounts with both God and your fellow man.

There are at least three ways to learn by mistakes. The best way is to read and follow God's Word and ways:

Thy word is a lamp unto my feet, and a light unto my path.
(Psalm 119:105)

I can only urge you to take that Bible route, and I guarantee you will never regret it!

A lesser way is to watch the errors of others to learn from them and take steps to avoid them. There was a lot I could have learned from my comrades and associates to be fair. Quite a few of them were finding themselves on the wrong side of the law.

I had one who was an international steroid dealer, for example. He sold a fortune worth of gear in the USA. That is highly illegal and a definite no-no. A Class 1 drug there at that point, while only a Class 3 here. Though not allowed for personal use in the USA, they were not illegal for personal use in the UK at that time. The FBI went undercover and sent him a one-way ticket promising him big rewards. (It's always worth rethinking the consequences when a one-way ticket lands on your doorstep!). Of course, he got put in jail and into a lot of trouble with it.

Yet another was involved in a police sting in Scotland. His case was dismissed and it was distinguished when he walked free due to police entrapment. His two co-accused received 9 years each for firearms offences. I was a witness on his behalf at the High Court. Sadly, he passed away later still as a young man under tragic circumstances.

The list goes on and on. One jailed for people trafficking, another charged with attempted murder and so on and so forth. Some were professional fighters yet that often brought them trouble. At times suffering relationship breakups, health issues and bad injuries. I had experienced a very badly torn pectoral muscle which was 90% detached. Still, I failed to take stock to check the balance as it were. The worst way to learn is to make those mistakes yourself. As a child touches a flame and smarts at the pain. He or she makes a mental note that hurts yet still suffers the burn that occurs. I refused the Word of God. Neither would I learn from my companions' glaring and obvious indiscretions. That only left one alternative, option 3: learn the hard way.

Remember our analogy of our friend the caterpillar? Growing big and doing harm? Or another way of putting it is becoming a big fish in a small pond. The problem is a big fish is not too hard to catch in that environment. Here is a verse that sums up this whole period better than any words I have:

"But we are all as an unclean thing, and all our righteousnesses are as filthy rags; and we all do fade as a leaf; and our iniquities, like the wind, have taken us away."
(Isaiah 64v6)

What a very sad verse. Yet it was an ever-so-accurate assessment of my life at that time.

CHAPTER 8
DEATH AND DESTRUCTION

AS THE FAMOUS IDIOM attributed to Sir Isaac Newton goes: "what goes up must come down" – and boy how it all came down, and so fast too! In this chapter, we will fast-forward a few years and hear how my life quickly unravelled. Yet I also invite you to think of Jesus' parable of the Prodigal son (Luke 15v11-32).

Even in his very worst moments, he was in his Father's mind. When he felt alone and undone, he was still loved and welcomed home – whether aware of it or not. I was also "a great way off". Yet looking back even on life's very darkest moments, I am now appreciative of a mother's love and prayers. Still more of my heavenly Father's care and protection. Many would have no longer recognised the wayward son. He must have smelt bad, been painfully thin and in dire straits. His Father knew him though. Far off as he was – he was his son!

The first crack to give out was the relationship I was in. It ended suddenly and badly. It knocked my confidence and gnawed away at me. Yet that was only the beginning of a stream of events that would each take a piece of me till all that remained was a broken man, in contrast to what I had been, as described at the beginning of my story.

I was spending quite a bit of my time in South East Asia. Thailand in particular was a place I spent a considerable stretch. It had great gyms, quality food and you could buy an unlimited amount of top-grade anabolic steroids over the counter in the pharmacies.

Many of the manufacturing factories were based there at that time too. It was the birthplace, of course, of Thai boxing which was of great interest to me too. It was a place in which I could earn money quite easily in the various activities I was involved in. Trouble was some of it was overseen by the Thai mafia who enviably wanted a cut in any action that was going on. The word 'no' was not an option!

My best and closest friend was a lad named Stewart. We were 'thick as thieves,' as they say. He was a good bit younger than me, at 27 years of age. He was a multi-titled word-class bodybuilder who had bags of wit and charm. Sad to say, in many ways, I introduced him to, or at least encouraged him in, the lifestyle he now led. He often spent time with me in the Far East. He had a reoccurring injury that was seriously hindering his career though. It caused downheartedness to set in. Still, we loved to party hard! Wild times numbed the pain at least at the time.

I remember the phone call from Stewart's dad: "Stewart is dead." That was it! Passed away in his sleep. What a tragedy; what a shock, and under the saddest of circumstances. I had been here before of course, but this brought it all flooding back. The pain and loss were searing! I honestly still miss him to this very day.

I had always been a happy go lucky type of guy. Never understood anyone who said they were depressed or could not lift their mood. For the first time, I found myself in just that situation. Despair had gripped me; it was deep and it was dark.

I contacted my second-best friend – a lad called Spencer who was thirty-four years old. I opened up to him and confided in him. I was struggling. He was in a similar 'line of work' as me. He also had many overseas contacts living in Spain for a time, working in Greece and frequently travelled to Russia where he had more than a nodding acquaintance with people involved in the Russian mafia. We arranged to meet in Newcastle. He was based in London and I, of course, was in Scotland. We had what I at that time would have thought of as a fantastic night. Today I would regard it as a shameful one.

We spoke a lot about what was going on in my life. Spencer brought some comfort to me as he reminded me "guys like you and I are top of the food chain, John – whatever you are going through, you will always bounce back." He must be right! I would just have to shake this feeling off. I would, in time, get over it.

We continued the party with the others he had brought along. One was head of airport security and the other an inspector with the government. Both were serious athletes too. That night they were just lads letting their hair down where all the usual vices and paraphernalia that were available.

Phone call number two came the following Friday. It was a London number but not Spencer's. "Hi John, Spencer has been found dead in a hotel room. They had to break down the door." He had taken a small quantity of recreational drugs – much less than we had taken the previous weekend. The doctors said it was the wrong dose on the wrong night.

You often find when you feel you have hit an all-time low that things cannot get any worse. They can, of course, when you continue down that same path.

Think of our prodigal. It started with a family rift. Still, he had cash. The cash went and with it the company. Bottomed out, but not really, for still to come was no food, shoes or obvious way back. I was now sure that, dark as things were, it could surely only get better. How wrong I was!

The next disaster was a business-related one which quickly escalated into a life-threatening situation. While I was in Thailand a top professional athlete who had very serious connections made a request that I deemed unreasonable and unacceptable. I said "No"! By all accounts no one I spoke to had come across a straight refusal before. What would he do? I would soon find out. I was informed I had to get out of the area immediately if I was to survive. I knew I could not go near an airport. They were no-go zones for me. The police in Thailand are not like here. They are easily bought off if you have the right contacts. Having done very little, you can find yourself on the wrong side of the law, with not a lot you can do about it.

At any rate, I made a phone call home to my mum. I explained it would be very difficult for me to leave that country and I may not be home for a long time if at all. What news for any mother to hear! My mum, however, seemed quite unperturbed. As I mentioned, she was a woman of faith. She said she and a group of her friends would pray for me – that God would bring me safety home and save me.

"You are not listening to me mum, I am not coming home. I can't be saved from this one." She calmly replied: "It is you who is not listening. I believe the Lord can save you and call you into the Christian ministry." I was flabbergasted, angry even. What a ridiculous suggestion!

A phone call was duly made to Thailand by another associate of mine who was a very heavy character (no longer with us), asking very nicely for my safe return as a personal favour. All parties involved knew what that meant. If I did not return safely there would be big trouble. The person whom I had my 'clash of heads' with over there was due a visit to Europe shortly afterwards and that would not be safe for him unless this was resolved to my friends liking. So, I left that country safely – but on one condition: I must never return. That was close! Still, I have lived to fight another day.

I decided that it would be best to lie low for a bit and stay in the UK till things blew over. I still spent a lot of time in North

East of England. This time I found myself in another highly dangerous situation and on this occasion I was innocent of the accusation levelled at me.

Strange how it all came out in the end. I was just so sick of all the problems that were cropping up that I decided to go for a day out down the coast on a bank holiday Monday in Whitley Bay with about twenty of my friends. It was always a party atmosphere on bank holidays and I had many a blowout there on previous occasions. I thought to myself "for this one day only I will put all my troubles behind me and have a good time."

I had showered, shaved and changed just ready to leave and was just about to put my jacket on when my mobile phone rang. Now, my first inclination was not to answer, but I did. A pal of mine asked me if I was going to a certain bar at a certain time. I confirmed I was.

"Don't go! There are guys waiting for you."

He mentioned who was involved, and I knew this was bad! This same friend was stabbed 14 times in a different incident. Thankfully he made a full recovery.

What had I done? Turns out a 'gangster' (for want of a better word), who already was not a fan of mine, got the information I had undercut him in a deal - which was not true. He has done a lot of jail since for very violent crimes. However, I had to leave again! Another place that was no longer safe for me.

Over in the book of Exodus you can read of ten plagues that came upon the Pharaoh and the Egyptians when they refused Gods ways and would not let the children of Israel go free (Exodus chapters 7-12). The first plague was *blood*. I could relate to that. The plagues progressively got worse till we get to number nine - *darkness*. This was followed by a tenth - *death*.

You may feel darkness is not so bad but this darkness was different:

> *"And the LORD said unto Moses, Stretch out thine hand toward heaven, that there may be darkness over the land of Egypt, even darkness which may be felt."* (Exodus 10:21)

I don't know if you have ever experienced darkness that may be felt but I now knew something of what that was. Everything seemed to be closing in but at least I still had my health and fitness. All was not lost, or so I imagined...

CHAPTER 9

A DEAL WITH THE DEVIL

I HAD A FEW OTHER bits and bobs of bother going on that were more local. One was with a builder who was crossing some lines with me and another with a world-class professional fighter. He was considerably lighter than I was but very much the real deal. That looked like inevitably coming to a head. They were certainly at the back of my mind but I was not overly concerned as I had been in this same type of position numerous times before. I was big and strong, could punch and kick, use my elbows and knees and was fairly competent at wrestling and on the deck (ground) too. I had trained with some of the best fighters around and thought whatever happens it's probably all been done to me before. I had been punched and kicked, head-butted, thrown and had much of the life choked out of me so often it felt like the norm. Rightly or wrongly, I concluded that a good big 'un should beat a good little 'un. Fortunately, I did not need to find out on that occasion.

Still, I did have some exciting things to look forward to. It was Friday tea time and the following day I was flying out to my house in Spain for a few days. Then next week I would be heading to the Philippines to my young sister Joanna's wedding. I had booked out the whole upstairs suite for myself and would be training with some great martial artists – masters in Filipino Kali – who were experts using the stick and knife. I would just get one last workout in before I went home and packed up. I had been fighting a few days earlier and my left knee was sore so I took some health supplements and strapped it up. It was a leg day in the weights and squatting was the order of the day. I did my first warm-up set and I felt stiff. Not to worry, perhaps it would loosen off as I progressed. I put more weight on and pushed ahead. It was a weight I was very capable of handling and had used for twenty plus years now. Nevertheless, I asked my training partner just to keep an eye on it. He was a great bodybuilder and a doctor as well. We trained together for fourteen years, four or five times a week. He passed away a few years ago at only fifty-two years of age. I carried that coffin too and think of him ever so often. Friends like that are hard to find and are sorely missed.

I did a few repetitions and then went a bit deeper. Boom! Something was seriously wrong here! I never experienced pain like it! My left leg had totally gone! All the weight went onto my other supporting leg. I pushed as hard as I could – Bang! It went too. I had torn right through both my quadricep tendons. The muscle that attaches your upper and lower legs. I momentarily passed out with the pain. I can remember everything ripping off and being stuck helpless at the bottom of a squat as my legs snapped forward against the joints and gave way. They say the bar locked on my neck and if Derek had not pulled it off it would have broken my neck. I just remember coming to, screaming for painkillers. Begging for them! Derek has also torn his bicep and chest, though not nearly as seriously, hauling it off me. An ambulance was duly called and felt like forever in arriving. They strapped me to a stretcher and lifted me in. They gave me an injection of some pain killer and gas and air till it kicked in as I recall.

The young doctor I was seen by in Accident and Emergency was a very pleasant chap but had not encountered that type of trauma before. He said it resembled a car crash injury. I told him I had torn off both tendons. He looked very sceptical and said only a consultant would know that for sure. It was a Friday evening and there was no one in that field there at that moment. Well, I am no consultant but turns out I was right enough! I remember when I tore my pectoral muscle, I said I doubted I would ever again experience pain like it. Well, that was like going to a party compared with the pain in my legs!

I was in the hospital for quite a time. First, the operation then next the recuperation and much later physio to help me walk again. They gave me very strong painkillers after it and I did not react to them well at all. They caused me to hallucinate and I remember one night calling my dad at 1.30 a.m. asking him to come to the hospital in a flat back truck to help me break free! The plan was to throw myself out of bed and onto the floor and crawl past the nurses and escape. I wanted him to use a quick cut stihl saw to cut off my plaster casts! Not the best plan I ever came up with to be fair. I had a plaster cast on both legs from my ankles to my hips and they were tied to the end of the bed. He called my mum and she came in and talked me around!

In the bed next to me was an old man who was making me extremely paranoid. He was sweet as honey during the day but was suffering from dementia. One night he was walking around my bed muttering, swearing and banging around my legs with his walking stick. I resolved if he got within distance to catch him. I could slip my hands around his neck and choke him unconscious. I knew many different ways to choke a person and was quite proficient at it. The aim is to close the carotid artery which causes a lack of blood in the brain and soon after that the person losses consciousness. I am so glad he did not come too close that night now though!

A group of ladies came into the hospital to visit me and pray for me. If ever a person needed prayer, I was that man. I vomited, burst out crying and they left. Like the journey of our caterpillar, I now felt like I was building a cocoon around myself. Partly for protection, partly I felt dying inside and ever-growing more aware great change was ahead. Like our prodigal, I was now in the pigpen. There is a saying: "youth is wasted on the young." Meaning that you have all the privileges of it and not the sense to use it wisely till it's too late. To be sure there is a bit of truth in that.

I was eventually allowed home to recuperate and given a special remote-control hospital bed that allowed me to raise and lower my back and my legs etc. I could not climb the stairs, shower myself or even put on socks without assistance. I was fitted with metal leg braces which were lowered an inch or two every month to allow more movement in my knees. It was a slow gruelling process. I felt ever so vulnerable. I had quite a few enemies and was now totally incapable of defending myself. My whole life had imploded and I knew it.

The despondency and gloominess felt overwhelming. I was far too ill to use recreational drugs now and never took a steroid from that day going forward. They cause your tendons and ligaments to weaken and were undoubtedly part of the problem with the injury I had sustained. My tendons were in tatters. I could feel bits of them floating around unconnected before they were surgically reattached. The surgeon said it was like trying to reconnect chicken to water!

Where to turn, though, that was the question. Christianity had never really done it for me and my lifestyle had kicked against it at every turn. I was "a great way off." I started to read books on self-help but the help I needed was definitely out with myself, I knew that. Then I read a few books on Buddhism but found no comfort there. If *karma* was true, I was in big trouble! There were no answers for me there.

I then started to contact fortune tellers and tarot card readers. It is a very dark thing to do and I warn you away from it in the strongest possible terms. Why? I wanted to know if things would get better. I was not in a relationship with God and did not hear from Him. Perhaps turning to the dark side may provide some answers?

I remember one night in particular feeling so low I just felt like I could not go on. I resolved to make a deal with the devil. I drew a circle around myself, wrote my name on a piece of paper and promised to sell my soul if I could have certain things back in my life. What a very dark and disturbing moment that still causes me to shudder as I ponder it.

I never did receive those things I asked for. I was not for sale, you see. I did not know that then of course.

> *"Forasmuch as ye know that ye were not redeemed with corruptible things, as silver and gold, from your vain conversation received by tradition from your fathers; But with the precious blood of Christ, as of a lamb without blemish and without spot."* (1 Peter 1:18-19)

A price had been paid for the soul of John MacInnes 2000 years ago! Paid in full, though I was still to realise it and walk in the good of it.

There is a very sad figure in the Old Testament I think about when I consider turning to the occult for answers. He was the first King of Israel and his name was Saul. (This Saul is not to be confused with the Saul, who became Paul, in the New Testament). King Saul had a grand start. He had favour with God and with men. Yet his wrong choices and unrepentant spirit caused him to end in the most tragic of circumstances. He no longer heard from God at all and turned to a witch who he asked to call up a spirit from the dead. The news he received brought him no comfort whatsoever. He was told he and his sons would die in battle the following day which did indeed happen. Do not dabble with the occult friends. You will not find the answers you are looking for there and it never ends well. (You will find this Bible story in 1 Samuel 28v3-25).

I felt on my own now. Nowhere really to turn. No way out. There is a verse in the Bible the sums up where I was at ever so well. In Romans 6:23 we read that, "*the wages of sin is death.*" It's like going to your work. You put in the shift earn your dues and at the end of a day, week or month you pick up what you have earned. Sin brings death. I did not need to be a theologian to affirm that. Friends going and gone; my own life in such great distress. Yet all that was happening was that I was collecting my dues. A blind man could have seen where it would all end, yet I was caught off guard. I never expected it or saw it coming. As always, the Word of God rings true.

Yet that is not where that verse in Romans 6 finishes. It continues: "*but the gift of God is eternal life through Jesus Christ our Lord.*" That could not possibly be true, could it? That through saving faith in Jesus Christ you no longer get what you deserve or have earned but you receive a 'gift' – something you have not worked for or earned; something that is eternal that cannot be taken from you; life in place of death and free access to God.

There was more than a glimmer of hope here and yet it seemed so far away. How could it be? Nothing short of a miracle was required for that to happen.

CHAPTER 10

THE MAN ABOVE THE MAN NEXT DOOR

MANY A DAY felt long and drawn out as I lay in bed recuperating. Family and friends popped in and out to feed me, walk my dog and check all was well.

I had a neighbour in the house across the road from me who regularly started to visit. His name was David, and he was a colourful very interesting character. I soon found out we had many common interests. This gentleman was a multitalented entrepreneur who was now semi-retired after having been a very successful businessman. In fact, at one point he bought a company with a respectable turnover and turned it into a household name while taking it up to a multi-million-pound turnover.

The business model used was very different though from either myself or any of my acquaintances. We were always looking for an angle. A way of getting around difficulties that can occur in buyouts and acquisitions. Ducking and diving was generally the order of the day! David, though, just did straight deals! No chicanery, nothing underhand- a pledge was given, a deal struck, his word was his bond and he stuck to it! What a novel idea. Yet it had worked. I was intrigued, to say the least. There was only one problem as far as I could see.

David was a devout Christian and often would speak to me about God. Great guy, I thought – but there is only so much about God I was willing to listen to. Yet here was my dilemma. I previously would have politely wound up our conversation and trotted off. Now I was in a bed with my legs tied to the end of it with nowhere to run (physically and metaphorically too). I was a captive audience so to speak! That said, he was never forceful or off-putting, which I had encountered before. The remarks made seemed almost casual yet were hard-hitting and thought-provoking.

My mum had recently given me a Bible for my birthday. That was acceptable but I had zero intention of actually picking it up or ever reading it. David too was a Bible-centred guy. What is wrong with everyone, I thought. My life was in ruins on every possible front and I get handed a Bible and a talk about it! They had no idea what I was going through. I had of course read parts from the Bible before many times. *"Thee,"* said this, and *"thou,"* said such and such. "Abraham begat Isaac" etc. How could that possibly help me now?

David (with our daughter Molly)
Spain, 2011

Still, I had one sitting next to my bed and all day to fill. I opened it up expecting very little and began to read. The Bible you see is like no other book. It is God's Word. A road map for your life and your eternal destination. You start reading it but find that very soon it is reading you. It points out your faults and failures and offers a solution and forgiveness. A relationship with God through His dear Son. I never expected that at all. Why did it feel different this time? Well, in all truth I had never really been open-minded previously. There were areas of my life I wanted to change and others that were 'no-go' areas!

Well, dear friend, you can never have a relationship with God while that is your attitude. He does not want a corner of your life, or to do a quick tidy-up job. He is in the business of deep change! He wants to access every area and is looking for a surrendered heart. That will never happen unless the Holy Spirit of God starts to move in your life. To give you understanding and illumination. To show you who you are and your deep need of Christ.

Many people claim to be searching for God. Yet my question is – How are you searching? If I lose a button or a coin, I search for it, I want to find it. Yet the reality is I can live without it. It would be nice to find – but not necessary. Many look for God in that manner. It would be nice to have Him in your life but the truth is you feel you can live just fine without Him.

Matthew 6v33 reads, *"Seek ye first the kingdom of God and His righteousness."* Not tenth or fifth, or even second – *above all* else seek after God. Now that is a very different attitude. It is seriously searching! *"And ye shall seek me, and find me, when ye shall search for me with all your heart"* (Jeremiah 29v13). You see, those who truly seek are promised they must find! God must honour that promise in His Word. If He fails to do so He is not to be trusted, not a keeper of His word and therefore not God at all. His honour is at stake and He won't pull out of His side of the bargain, not even when it is at His own cost! It is a matter of urgency for you above all else to get right with Him on His terms. It is a matter of the heart.

One thing I find strange, looking back, is where I started to read. As a minister, I generally advise people to start in one of the gospels. Perhaps Mark or John. Now of course the whole Bible is God's Word and of equal validity. We read in 2 Timothy 3v16-17:

"All scripture is given by inspiration of God, and is profitable for doctrine, for reproof, for correction, for instruction in righteousness: That the man of God may be perfect, throughly furnished unto all good works."

That said, some parts are more challenging than others. I did not start in the gospels or even in the New Testament. Neither did I start in the first book of the Bible - Genesis (beginnings). I started in the book of Daniel! It is a very prophetic book and certainly one that even mature Christians can wrestle with. Yet I just felt as I read it the words were jumping off the page at me. It is the story of a man with quite a privileged background who was taken against his will to a place he would never have chosen but even there when everything seemed stacked against him started to get an overwhelming desire to pray and connect with God. I could relate to that! What is more, God spoke to him and so I concluded He could speak to me! I actually (mistakenly of course) started to think I just understood everything that the book was talking about. Yet I tell you this much - I was understanding what I needed to understand at that time. Blinded eyes were starting to open, and as Jesus once said to a scribe of all people in Mark's gospel: *"thou art not far from the kingdom of God."*

Another spiritual exercise came alongside reading and that was prayer. Not some religious words or anything committed to memory. Not even something I had heard or read. Just a cry out to God from the dark. A desire to get to know Him. An understanding that without Him I had no hope or future.

The strange thing about all of this is that not a single person had any idea this was going on. I did not share it with a soul and kept it secret. Outwardly it was very difficult to spot. Before of course I would have been living a wild lifestyle but now it was very subdued by necessity. I had previously and repeatedly tried to clean up my life often but always hit the same hurdle. If, for example, I wanted to take fewer drugs I would force myself to do so for a time. Yet the big problem was that the desire was still there. When the Holy Spirit starts to work in you not only are you no longer doing the things you once did but the desire to do them goes too! *"Therefore if any man be in Christ, he is a new creature: old things are passed away; behold, all things are become new"* (2 Corinthians 5v17). New desires, a new way of thinking and a brand new life!

As I started slowly to recover, I spent quite a bit of time with David. He influenced many areas of my life, mentoring and encouraging me. I was not yet fully through for Christ at this stage but a definite work of grace was starting in my life. I was very aware of it.

But what of the 'Man' above? Please be assured I do not use that term disrespectfully or flippantly. Pontius Pilate the Roman Governor who condemned Jesus to crucifixion once made a very gripping statement as Christ stood before Him. *"Then came Jesus forth, wearing the crown of thorns, and the purple robe. And Pilate saith unto them, Behold the man!"* (John 19v5). Question: What do you see as you look at Christ? Pilate said, *"Behold the man."* Yet he failed to recognise Him as other-worldly, from above. Look at Christ through the eyes of faith and you will see God manifest in the flesh. A Saviour reaching out to the lost. I never saw it till then but stage by stage my blinded eyes were starting to open. Recognition and appreciation of this were fast growing in me; a desire to know Him above all else.

Becoming a Christian is more than a decision you make. It is nothing less than a supernatural encounter with the Living God. Could that be what had been missing in my life? Was it a person and not a thing? Was it a spiritual need even more than my obvious emotional and physical needs? When Jesus encountered Nicodemus in John 3 and explained the necessity of the new birth, the old Pharisee said in astonishment: *"How can these things be?"* John MacInnes, the athlete, the businessman who had been heading down an ever-narrowing and darkening path was soon to find out.

CHAPTER 11
TWO BLIND DATES

ONE DICTIONARY DEFINITION of 'blind date' I read described it as, "a social appointment or date arranged, usually by a third person, between two people who have not met." Well, I was about to have two of them! But let's not jump the gun…

I was now starting to recover to the point I could again walk. I would soon need to consider working again. I had no idea what I would do but I did know this much: that I wanted to leave that old lifestyle behind and move away from it.

David had put his house up for sale and had an offer accepted on it. I would be sad to see him move away, that was for sure. One morning I unexpectedly heard a call from my front door. It was David. In a cheery tone, he shouted in: "how would you like to buy my house? I will sell it to you for a good price!"

(Me): "I thought you had sold it?"

(David): "It fell through."

(Me): "Definitely not; I have no available funds right now."

(David) "I will just drop in price till you say yes, I want to sell it today"

(Me): "I won't say, yes."

Well, he dropped the price and I said 'yes'! Next, a phone call to the bank to raise the finance for it. Now the big question – What would I do with it? Property prices were booming in Scotland at that time. I had recently bought and sold a property I lived in briefly and made a handsome sum on it. I had something of an eye for spotting old buildings and renovating them to make a profit. Should be able to do that with this one, I thought. It was certainly the right price.

Deal done, monies transferred and then unexpectedly within weeks the whole economy went into a recession very few saw coming! It seemed like a bit of a disaster. Now, what would I do? It was a fairly large building and I came up with a plan of opening a few of the rooms as a guest house just to cover the mortgage till things picked up. I had never done that line of work before but was willing to give it a try.

David's wife Betty was a bit of a matchmaker. "Would you like me to introduce you to a girl? "Absolutely not," I thought. I knew the type of girls I liked and was pretty sure Betty had never met one and would certainly not introduce me to one! Still, what had I to lose? I had been house-bound now for months and it was only a few short steps over to their home. OK – a blind date! Who would have thought it!

They introduced me to a girl called Danielle. She was entirely different from my usual type.

Danielle was a Christian for one thing. I hobbled over and shared a carryout meal with them. She was a beautiful,

My lovely wife, Danielle with your's truly

intelligent and interesting girl. Later I would seek out her phone number and give her a call.

We caught up for a bite to eat and I remember I could not walk up the one flight of stairs to the restaurant but had to take the lift! One question I asked was: "do you use a lot of drugs?" She looked at me as if I was quite mad. She responded by telling me she had never taken a drug in her life. How strange, I thought. "What do your friends say about that?" None of her friends used drugs either.

This was quite bizarre as almost all of my friends did! How I ever got another date I will never know!

Now many people when they come to Christ have a special moment – a time and place where they can say for sure they were born again. Like the apostle Paul on the Damascus Road in Acts 9. My own experience seemed much more gradual, more of a journey back, like our young prodigal. My life was radically different now yet I had still not been to church. Health was one of the reasons for that, but not the only one.

The little guest house was starting to come to life with six bedrooms for rent. I met a very interesting old man from the USA. He was from a very sheltered Mennonite background. At ninety years of age, he was not fit to be travelling alone. He was just handing out his bank card to anyone he could find, giving them his PIN number and asking them to withdraw cash and bring it to him. I involved the police who came and visited me. They contacted his family in the USA. They wanted him to return home. His name was Roy and he was adamant he wanted to finish this trip to Scotland before he died. He was researching his family history and Scotland was a big adventure on his 'bucket list'. Somehow or other I ended up giving my word I would look after him during his stay. It seemed a pretty Christian thing to do to me at any rate. Perhaps I could help him. I never imagined for a second it was Roy who would help me.

We had never spoken a word about faith till that point but I was having a private battle and felt in turmoil. We were driving along with him in the back seat and I was wrestling with my thoughts. What could I do from here on in? The old life was not an option. I knew that. I silently prayed this prayer: "Lord shew me a way." That was it. But I meant it.

Roy leaned over and asked me:

"Do you know the love chapter in the Bible, 1 Corinthians 13?"

"Sorry I don't know much about that," I replied.

He asked if I had any interest in the Bible and I said I had recently become very interested in it. He boldly said, "the last verse in 1 Corinthians 12 before that love chapter says *'and yet I shew unto you a more excellent way.'*" He just felt he should share that, he said. He had no idea of the significance of what he was saying to me, but I did. That was my prayer: "Show me a way." God's immediate reply came in this word: *"I shew you a more excellent way"!* He has, you know, yes, He has!

The property I had recently purchased was called Kidron House. Now Kidron is a Bible name (see 1 Kings 15v13; John 18v1). I opened more rooms until we had 15 at one point and a restaurant to serve our guests and people from the village too.

Formerly our Hotel – Kidron House

That first year was a hard one, in all honesty. I did a lot of the work myself. Washing towels, frying eggs – you name it. I should perhaps have mentioned I was a decent cook and had taken one-to-one lessons for a couple of years from a friend of mine who was then a TV chef and had worked in some pretty plush places in London, where he is based at the time of writing this book.

I had another friend working with me. He did not speak any English but solely Spanish. 'Angel' is his name! He pulled out all the stops to help me that first year. The communication barrier was a problem for the other staff but was great practice for me. Anyway, cutting to the chase, I worked ever so hard that year to earn but a fraction of my previous income. It did not matter one little bit though as it was honest money, and without the problems that the old way of life had so often brought me.

David had asked me along to church many times. I thought, 'OK, I will go one time and then he never needs to ask me again.' Now, although the Lord was real in my life, I was also aware I had a bad reputation in my local area. What would people think if I was to walk into their church? Well, I went along very tentatively but was overwhelmed by the welcome I received. The people just made me feel like I was part of a family. I had worked in a big nightclub around the corner and had part-owned a trendy bar in that town. I thought for sure my reputation would proceed me. No one mentioned it.

So many questions: Was I comfortable? Would I like tea? How are you today? I would love to see you back, etc. Many were elderly, but as I previously mentioned, I like the older company. There was no judgment, just genuine concern. If you ask someone to church and they don't go the first time, don't despair. Perhaps like myself, they are struggling with it, weighing up the cost while the Holy Spirit works in them. Remember the Prodigal Son's return?

> *"But the father said to his servants, Bring forth the best robe, and put it on him; and put a ring on his hand, and shoes on his feet: And bring hither the fatted calf, and kill it; and let us eat, and be merry: For this my son was dead, and is alive again; he was lost, and is found. And they began to be merry."* (Luke 15v22-24).

I was now living in the good of it!

Now to that second blind date. Writing to a young Christian called Timothy, Paul wrote: *"For there is one God, and one mediator between God and men, the man Christ Jesus"* (1 Timothy 2v5). Remember our dictionary definition of blind date again: ..."a social appointment or date arranged, usually by a third person, between two people who have not met." If you are seriously looking to find God today it can only happen through an intermediary connecting both of you. That is, the Lord Jesus Christ. He is not just a *good* way to do that or even the *best* way. He is the *only* way! To one of His close disciples, Thomas, we read that *"Jesus saith unto him, I am the way, the truth, and the life: no man cometh unto the Father, but by me"* (John 14v6). I found Christ to be the 'missing link' between God and man. A date with destiny for sure – a date with the previously unknown God.

Chapter 12
TYING THE KNOT

DANIELLE AND I were getting on ever so well. We arranged to be married at the church we had started to attend. Danielle reminded me as I am writing this chapter that I said on one of our early dates that I would write a book someday and call 'our chapter' *Blind date*! Please believe me when I tell you that that was said tongue in cheek. I had no intention, or the ability for that matter, to write any book. Yet here I am some 13 years later doing just that!

I was encouraged to go along to church regularly before getting married. I was happy to do so but can recall one particular sermon above all others. The truth is, I don't recall much of what was preached in the first church I attended as a Christian. Yet, I have fond memories of my time there. They showed us a lot of love and at that time that was what I needed in my life. This message though was from the letter to Philemon in the New Testament. It is the story of a runaway slave and the apostle Paul asks his previous master to permit his return and treat him as a brother with love. Total forgiveness was the request. That tugged at my conscience quite a bit. Some people I could easily forgive and reconcile with. Others would be more challenging. I soon realised the necessity of forgiving and also over the years of seeking the forgiveness of others I had wronged.

Now, you must remember that some will accept your apology and wish you the best. There are others still not in a good place themselves or whom you have deeply wounded who perhaps will not or cannot at that time. You still have a duty to keep your side of the road clear and do as much as you can to rectify any wrongs. Those 'good works' certainly won't save you but they do prove a genuine work of grace has taken place in your life. God does not let you off the hook with such a huge area as unforgiveness, even if you are not fully aware of it.

One person in particular immediately sprung to mind. A nasty piece of work from my past who had been bullying a few people I knew and trying to extort money from them. I had recently heard he had broken an old man's arm. I knew a family he was terrorising with a disabled child too, causing them misery and great financial pressure. Finally, he started treading on my toes! I won't go into the detail of it but let us say this much – that did not end well for him and it's likely to have been an experience he would not have quickly forgotten. I felt very bad toward him. I am not proud to admit that some of my actions in the past have changed people's lives for the worse. Today I endeavour, through God's Word and my testimony, to change lives for the better.

No way did he deserve forgiveness. He was not a bit sorry for what he did and from what I heard, though he now stayed away from me, he continued to pressurise and blackmail people. However, neither had I deserved forgiveness but now I had been fully pardoned by God. I prayed for him regularly after that, asking God to bless him and change him. Soon afterwards I heard he passed away. I don't know much of the details of it and never had an opportunity to speak with him again. The truth is I don't know if he changed or not, but I do know that through praying for him I did. It is very difficult to hold bitterness towards a person while going before God praying for them. The bitterness goes, and with it you find freedom in yourself.

It's a funny thing as I recall how that progressed. It started by praying God would give me a heart to forgive him (though secretly I thought God knows everything, therefore he knows what he is like and probably realises he is a bad one!). Then I prayed He would change him (because God changes bad people!). Finally, I prayed God would bless him (though at first, I thought it would be pretty hard to swallow if He did it!). Finally, as I prayed I found myself meaning it.

Often, we look at people and see their character flaws while having little insight as to the process they have been through to get to that place. Perhaps a terrible childhood or a trust broken, an illness you know nothing of or a death that is causing secret grief. Jesus, we are told, knew what was in the heart of man; we on the other hand do not.

Another relationship that needed working on from my end was with my dad. I had fallen out with him and not spoken for quite a time. That had to be corrected to move on and be at peace both with him and God. My dad came to our wedding shortly after that. He now regularly attends the church I preach at and our relationship is so much better. I love my dad and am thankful for how he has provided for me and supported me in my life in many ways. I can think of a few occasions I was delighted to have him in my corner as a youth. Once when I was around fourteen an old farmer shot our dog dead and shot at me too (shotgun full of salt pellets in my case). As I recall he was a strange old character and ended up in jail for shooting off a child's hand! To be fair I was ploughing through his fields on a motorbike I had bought for the price of an old coffee jar full of loose change! My dad went around and 'sorted him out!' The rest, as they say, is history!

When I was around fifteen an older man asked me for a fight. My dad was having none of it! He assured me he would have to fight him first! He could be quick off the mark at times yet at other times he could show self-control.

I recall when I was ten years old playing a game called 'wallie'. If you are not from Scotland, I had best explain what that is. It involves kicking a football against a wall and hitting it while it bounces back. I was always a terrible football player, but in 1978 Scotland was in the World Cup and every young boy was football mad. My dad came out of the house and asked me to stop kicking the ball, saying I would break the kitchen window. I had been at it for about an hour and said I would not. The next shot the ball crashed straight through the window! Glass everywhere. My dad was pretty measured in his response to be fair!

He was proud of what I had achieved throughout my life. He attended competitions when I was an athlete, was delighted with what I achieved in business, and though our relationship has had its ups and downs I have always loved him and been sure he loves me too.

Who would ever have imagined I would be preaching in the pulpit and my dad sat in the pew? He came to my ordination and openly wept at it. Now, that is a miracle and one I am deeply humbled and thankful for. He recently sent me a card telling me he loves me and is so pleased with where I am at today.

> *"And I will restore to you the years that the locust hath eaten, the cankerworm, and the caterpillar, and the palmerworm, my great army which I sent among you. And ye shall eat in plenty, and be satisfied, and praise the name of the LORD your God, that hath dealt wondrously with you: and my people shall never be ashamed."* (Joel 2:25-26).

Sometimes we can all be guilty of reading the scriptures yet missing the real-life applications. This Old Testament passage speaks of restoration. Wasted years being compensated for. God dealing in wonder-working power in lives and shame being taken away. I can testify to the veracity of these verses and have known something of what it is to walk in the goodness of them.

Well, we were married on 20th December 2009! It was a day to remember indeed. My wife looked radiant (she still does). It was such a happy occasion. One of my old friends from my past was my best man. He used to describe himself as a gangster, but a nice one! Others were my ushers. I love every one of those guys. The truth is they stuck by me through thick and thin and we have a lot of history. I want to see them won for Christ today.

David sat at the top table beside me. My sisters were all present with my mum. Danielle and I even learned a special routine for our first dance and told no one about it till they saw us on the day. It went down a storm, funny looking back on it now.

Just over nine months later our first daughter - Molly Anne MacInnes was born. What a change and how quickly it had all happened. Two years later our son Murdo John MacInnes would follow too. The Lord has been so very gracious to us. I love my wife and our children. I often wake up in the early hours of the morning with Danielle beside me and the kids next door. I cannot help but think how very different my life is today.

Just after our marriage, I also met up with a 'big name' from the circles I was previously involved in. I bumped into Charles working in a tile store. He had a huge reputation in our area having lived a life of crime and working as an enforcer within a very serious well-known gang. He had become a Christian now too and over the years we have become the very best of friends. A gentler soul with a heart for people you will not meet. He has the heart and gifting of an Evangelist and regularly works with those in addiction. He has seen many won for Christ. I never knew it then but he was praying for a Christian friend he could walk with and do life with. We have often prayed together, preached together and reached out for Christ as a team.

Remember our old dying caterpillar as it entered into the cocoon it was making for itself? It looks very unlikely to emerge from it - yet it does. Everything about it is changing in that place. How it looks, what it sees, its appetites. You just never know what God is doing under the surface of a person's life. Never write them off. God is a God of miracles - of the impossible:

"Behold, I am the LORD, the God of all flesh: is there anything too hard for me?" (Jeremiah 32v27).

20th December, 2009
Our big day!

Chapter 13
IT'S A PLEASURE TO SERVE

ONE THING I ENCOURAGE every Christian to do is get involved in some type of service or ministry for the Lord as soon as possible. There are various reasons I say this:

Firstly, we all should do it as we are commanded to do, and have a biblical mandate to do so.

Also, for anyone who has been involved with an ungodly type of lifestyle or one where a large part of their day has been taken up in an unsavoury manner, one problem is when you remove these things there is a huge hole in your day.

It is therefore wise to fill it with positives to replace the negatives.

Now, what exactly do I mean by 'ministry'? In 1 Timothy 3v6 we read: *"Not a novice, lest being lifted up with pride he fall into the condemnation of the devil."* This passage speaks clearly of church leadership and only those that are mature in their Christian faith qualify for it. You may feel ready and be keen as mustard – but you have to learn to stand before you can walk and walk before you can run. It is a time to learn and not to teach.

That said, although the bible so wisely nurtures and protects young Christians from church office there are various examples of people going straight to work for Jesus. Remember the woman at the well (John 4)? She held no official position but immediately run back to her town and told the men who had been in her life about her encounter with Christ (John 4v28-29). The result was a mini-revival in that town (v39)!

Or what of the mad man among the tombs (Mark 5v1-20)? He wanted to go with Jesus on the boat. Instead, Jesus told him to go into the ten surrounding cities of Decapolis and tell what great things the Lord had done for him. Testimony and evangelism are permitted and encouraged at the earliest opportunity. It may be in your home or among your friends. There is no more powerful testimony to a changed life than to those who know you well.

The question is what can you do? It is a sad inditement on our churches that often it is the same few willing souls who do the lion's share of the service while others are little more than spectators. Don't be a consumer my friend - get active for Christ and do it now! What can you do to help? To further His cause and kingdom? What are your burdens? The things you pray over, the things that interest you? Do you like working with children? Are you good with computers, is your background in finance? Can you teach? Are you musical? Are you an academic or streetwise? Are you a background person or a people person? God often uses our past experiences as He calls us to service.

For myself, I also found an unexpected benefit in serving others after a lifetime of placing my own needs and fancies first. I found it was good to give back and not just take. To reach out to those who needed help just as people had so lovingly done for me. I started with a desire to give out but soon became a beneficiary of doing so.

When I now consider how ministry began for me, I must confess at the time I did not have a clue that is even what it was. We had a breakfast club in the church I attended on Mondays and Fridays. It was run by some of the very nicest of people who gave freely of their time to help serve those caught up in the addiction lifestyle. Some of the older ladies were ever so kind - but not always the most streetwise! The first Monday I walked in it was like a drug dealers paradise. People were scoring deals while the food was being served.

Now you would think nothing of my past life could help prepare me for ministry. As I mentioned I had been a nightclub bouncer for a while. One thing I could spot was drug deals going down as well as those heavily under the influence of them. That is useful to know as once you are aware of the type of drug it is easier to gauge how a person might behave.

For example, those on opiates - heroin and the like - can 'gouch', or fall asleep. It is a serious addiction that often drives those souls caught up in it to go to great lengths to get their next fix. Lying and stealing often become the norm. That said, they are generally not aggressive unless they feel a reason to be so. Amphetamines, or cocaine, are a very different type of drug with people full of energy and chat running ahead at full pelt till they often crash out. It can easily lead to a lifestyle of uppers and downers just to try and get on an even keel.

This may surprise you, but the most unpredictable of all is alcohol. A person can be your best friend and want to hug you one minute yet hit you the next! For that reason, we kept a close but friendly eye on what was going on with no bottles or potential weapons allowed. On a Friday a retired Police Inspector served the breakfasts. Jim was very much on the ball and we quickly got into a routine working together. Today we are very close friends and Jim and his wife, Alison, have supported us in so many different ways in our lives. Both have a heart for God and a heart to serve. They have been a great example and encouragement to me personally throughout the years.

My role was to distribute the food as well as on occasion prepare it. Cooking was fine but I enjoyed just getting in among our friends and serving them a hot meal and chatting with them. At first many were closed books and only wanted to eat. Yet as time went on and we developed trust and mutual respect a bond was formed and they would often share details of their lives. I prayed with many a person in that food hall. I have mopped up sick, stacked the chairs and swept the floor.

That was my introduction to ministry. I was learning how to show love and connect and reach out for Christ. Over the years that experience has stood me in good stead. As we read in the gospels: *"He that is faithful in that which is least is faithful also in much: and he that is unjust in the least is unjust also in much"* (Luke 16v10). If you are unwilling to serve and be trustworthy in a small area, how can you possibly expect God to trust you with more?

I have encountered a few young men over the years ever so eager to preach. There is nothing wrong with that if God has that call on your life. It will happen in time. Don't be over-keen or try to push it or self promote. Let God promote you if He will. As we read in the Book of Proverbs: *"A man's gift maketh room for him, and bringeth him before great men"* (Proverbs 18v6). If God has given you a gift it will show and others will recognise it too. If man promotes you, he can also decommission you – if God promotes you no one can hold you back.

Around this time Danielle and I started to listen to services online from a well known church in Northern Ireland, Whitewell Metropolitan Tabernacle. Pastor James McConnell was the senior pastor at that time. My sister Christine attended but I had never been there or even seen Pastor McConnell. We started to listen every Sunday evening together. Soon I was buying the CDs and listening to sermons every day.

I listened to a sermon a day every day for a year! Often 3 or 4 a day! No one knew that then. The teaching was of a high standard and I was aware it was helping me to grow spiritually. The church we first attended was having some internal issues and sadly some things came up which I could not in good conscience agree with. We then attended a church in Glasgow for a little while where a minister I knew to be a servant of Christ was the preacher. William was very kind to us and I am forever grateful for our time there. We are still friends to this day and I hold him in the highest respect.

At that point, our link with Whitewell was growing. I eventually went over and was made welcome. My idea was to slip in unnoticed and slip out again, though it never ended up being like that. Again, it was how friendly and outreaching the people were that initially caught my attention. Many aspects of their ministries resonated with us. I was asked to give my testimony at a house meeting of one of the Pastors and from there friendships developed and grew.

Now, the truth is I was hungry for God. I wanted more of Him. I was aware they were having a series of meetings on Monday evenings seeking a deeper experience of God. I wanted that and, though only my wife knew, I determined somehow to get from Scotland to Belfast each Monday searching for a deeper encounter with God. I would finish my work and get a cheap deal over on the ferry as a foot passenger returning later the same evenings.

Monday, 26th March 2012, was a day that I will not easily forget. Pastor McConnell preached one verse before coming down and praying with anyone who wanted more of Christ and a fresh touch of the Holy Spirit. Call it what you will, but I wanted to be emptied of self and filled with God. Psalm 72v6, was the verse that evening: *"He shall come down like rain upon the mown grass: as showers that water the earth."* As I heard the text I got excited and a hunger welled up in my soul. Even before anyone prayed with me the power of God fell on me in a way I had never before experienced. In the book of Acts, you read how 120 were in an upper room praying and reading the scriptures. Suddenly, the Holy Spirit fell on those people and they went into the streets at 9 a.m. with a boldness they had not experienced before. The result was that 120 became 3120 within the day (Acts 1v15; 2v41). That, my friends, is revival! That is the difference when God's Spirit falls on a place.

There is an old preacher who was mightily used in the 1949 Lewis revival named Duncan Campbell. You can still access some of his sermons to this day. Often he used the phrase "when God stepped down." You immediately sense it is more than a notion or something he has read about. He was there when it happened and was greatly used by the Lord. We need God to fill people today and for those who have experienced the life and power of God to share it with the multitude.

When God empowers anyone, it is never for some selfish motive. It is for service for Him. When you have been a servant to sin it is the most liberating experience in the world to become a servant of Jesus.

Chapter 14

CHALLENGE AND CHANGE

WE STARTED to have prayer meetings in our home on a very regular basis. Charles met with me most mornings for an hour and other lads came along at various times and seasons. These morning daily times of prayer went on for several years. We still to this day have a prayer meeting early each Friday morning as well as catching up throughout the week.

We also started a small prayer meeting on a Thursday evening. It began with a couple of us but over months people just kept coming along. Most were not even locals with some travelling well over an hour just to reach us. We soon had to move out of our living room to a large room we had downstairs where we could seat up to around forty people. Within months it was full and folks were squeezing in next to each other with overspill into the kitchen at times too. We crammed seventy in one night as I particularly recall.

We had no intention of starting a church but all of a sudden we found ourselves to be involved in just that – a church plant, though at the birthing and baby stages for sure. We invited various speakers to come along, as I was not yet preaching at that stage. Some of my friends in ministry were ever so helpful in lending a hand in those early meetings and encouraging us.

Pastor David, whose house meeting I had spoken at in Northern Ireland, offered to come over with Pastor

McConnell. That made me quite nervous to be honest, as Pastor McConnell was used to speaking to thousands at a time and here we were just a very small group yet with enthusiasm and excitement for the things of God, and what was happening among us. They duly came, as promised, and after a memorable evening, we felt led to arranging a Sunday service.

We looked for a suitable premise and the Grand Hall, Kilmarnock, came up as a particularly attractive option. It is a very well-known building within our community. It is next to the bus station and close to the train station. It had different sizes of rooms and they were flexible permitting us to move as and when required.

On Thursday 25th July 2013 we organised an evangelical outreach at which Pastor McConnell was the speaker. I would share my testimony at it. We had no idea how many would come along but we kept inviting people and covering the event in prayer. Five hundred people came along that night! It was obvious for all to see God that was at work in this.

Sunday services became regular after that, with a weekly service as well as a Thursday evening prayer meeting. Pastor McConnell kindly permitted Pastor David to help us get set up. The numbers then were greatly reduced for a time as many had their own Sunday service to attend. That said, a core group had now thrown in their lot. I am ever so grateful as I look back at the kindness and assistance that was afforded to us at that time. For the next couple of years, I was mentored and encouraged as I became more deeply involved in ministry. I recall the first time I was asked to speak and was given a fifteen-minute slot to share. My first thought was – that sounds like a long time! What can I say! Still, I took it very seriously and learned and grew. Even then I was aware of a call to ministry. Yet there was an inner struggle going on. A desire to reach people for Christ but with little from my past to qualify me to do that.

For all the things I had done in my past life, public speaking was one that I had managed to avoid and the thought of it filled me with dread. The apostle Paul felt the same conflict, which is comforting. He said, "*who is sufficient for these things?*" He also said, "*Woe is me if I preach not the gospel.*" There is the tension, but what to do?

In Paul's second letter to Timothy he encourages the young preacher: "*Study to shew thyself approved unto God, a workman that needeth not to be ashamed, rightly dividing the word of truth*" (2 Timothy 2v15). It was a time to study, to soak up what I could and make myself available, then to leave the results to the Lord. Not too long afterwards I started doing a lot more of the preaching. Yet I had a hunger for a deeper knowledge of the word.

For the first time, I considered Bible College. That would be difficult for many reasons. My son Murdo was not long since born and I was trying to spend time with my family. I was also very busy in the hotel as it had grown into a busy business and I was now studying and preaching regularly too. It seemed barely sensible or even possible to put something else into the mix. Yet I knew it would be beneficial for me in my spiritual development. I had no clue where I might go either. I prayed a very short prayer which went something like this: "Lord if you want me to go to Bible College please show me where to go."

My sister Joanna, who is a missionary, was in the UK for a short visit at that time but I had no idea where she was. The prayer was no sooner out of my mouth than I heard a ping on my mobile phone as a text came through. It was Joanna, and she said: "Hi, we are in Wales at a Bible College. It's a very special place. I think you should consider visiting it!" What a remarkable response to prayer. Many a prayer I am still waiting to be answered, others were answered over time – but not that one! It was immediate.

Within the week I drove the four hundred and fifty miles down with my family and met with the Principal Dr Colin Hurt. I explained my predicament and the problem of entering into full-time study. But I had a desire to learn. Dr Hurt offered a solution which was to spend one week in Scotland with my family and church while also overseeing the hotel and the next week studying in Wales. I could return home at the weekends. I could continue my studies over two sessions – even three if necessary. This is exactly what I did. There were times I felt stretched to the limit, yet throughout it all, I was ever so grateful and felt blessed by this great privilege of the opportunity.

The BCW (Bible College of Wales) was another huge and positive influence in my life. It was opened by a group of Singaporean Christians who wanted to sow into the UK and the nations. Pastor Yang and his wife Daphne were the lead persons and I just loved my time there. I try to get back at least once each year to spend a quiet week in prayer and contemplation. It is an opportunity to catch up with old friends while recharging my spiritual batteries so to speak, as well as sitting in on any new lecturer or subject I have not encountered there before. They brought in some great teachers and the curriculum was just what I needed. I met many Christians from the persecuted church and friends at all stages of ministry. As the Word tells us: *"iron sharpens iron,"* meaning being among like-minded people keeps you sharp. That it did.

Many a Sunday I would preach at church in Scotland finishing around 1 p.m. I would change out of my suit, kiss my wife and kids and head straight down to Swansea with a packed lunch listening to sermons and praying most of the way there. I would arrive exhausted but contented around 10 p.m. ready for our studies early Monday morning. When the week ended on Friday at 1 p.m. I was back in the car and heading home again! It was challenging, but I believe it was character building at the same time.

Going back to the hotel was becoming ever more difficult for me. My mind was elsewhere. It was becoming less important to me each week. I was now the wrong man to be at the helm as my heart was elsewhere. I had a burden for souls now and I knew it was not going away. Yet I had responsibilities to my wife and children, to support them, and to the staff who were so faithful to me.

I recall one morning being impressed by scripture as I read it, Matthew 4v18-20: *"And Jesus, walking by the sea of Galilee, saw two brethren, Simon called Peter, and Andrew his brother, casting a net into the sea: for they were fishers. And he saith unto them, Follow me, and I will make you fishers of men. And they straightway left their nets, and followed him."*

It spoke of men with commitments being called into full-time ministry by Jesus. Immediately they left everything and followed Him. I felt the draw of that was becoming overwhelming. I knew it was the call of God, but how could that be possible? I had financial and business obligations as well as people depending on me for one thing, it seemed preposterous just to leave all that without much thought and rejigging of my life. I shared my dilemma with Charles and we prayed about it. My mind was working overtime just weighing it all up and I returned home and spoke about it with Danielle. I remember saying to her that I just wanted to lay it down for a bit, and I was going to take an hour off and listen to a live online service. Danielle was right behind me and fully involved with that ministry decision and has also been fully supportive in so many ways since.

I tuned into Pastor McConnell preaching. He of course had no clue what I was going through. He opened by saying "Let's turn to Matthew Chapter 4, verses 18-20"! I could not believe it! He then preached a sermon that made me very uncomfortable. Obedience to the calling of Christ. He looked straight at the screen and boldly announced "delayed obedience is disobedience. He wants you now!"

I was not sure how any of this could work out even if I was given a long period to try to do it. I did know, however, that I did not want to put off one more day and would trust God to work out the details. I called in my staff the next morning for a meeting and explained where I was at. I then said: "You guys are looking for money but I am looking for time. If we can structure a deal you can take over the running of the hotel if I can have time for ministry." I agreed to come in a couple of hours a week to deal with the essentials. We shook hands and just as quick as that I was free to pursue the call of God on my life.

Thankfully, we are not called to know all the details of what the Lord will do as He asks us to step out in faith. We are, however, called to be obedient and trust Him to do the rest. There is a very famous chorus called 'Trust and obey.' It is said that while a well-known evangelist by the name of Dwight L. Moody was preaching a young man rose to his feet in the meeting and declared "I am not quite sure how, but I am going to trust and obey." A member of the choir scribbled down his words on a piece of paper and a Presbyterian minister by the name of Rev. J. H. Sammis (1846-1919) penned the words of that now famous hymn some 143 years ago. The chorus goes like this

Trust and obey,
For there's no other way
To be happy in Jesus,
But to trust and obey.

I have no better advice to offer you, dear friends.

CHAPTER 15

VISITATION, GRADUATION AND ORDINATION

THERE ARE SEASONS as a Christian in which your desires for spiritual things intensify; times you just want more of God. This was such a season. The Bible College of Wales was set up by a famous Welsh evangelist and intercessor named Mr Rees Howells (1879-1950). His life is worth reading up on if you never have before, and there are a variety of good books to choose from should you so wish. It is a stately home on a grand estate. It had been sadly left derelict for many years until taken over and recommissioned for God's work. The gardens are magnificent and I spent many an early morning or late evening seeking God in them. There were various nooks and crannies to hide away in. There is an old well for example in a very peaceful spot that was covered over for many years. I met a very old godly man named Brian who had been a student there decades before. He recalled a very powerful story of how he had met with God at that well. He never revealed the content of that encounter but I do know that on the strength of it he immediately sold up all his possessions and moved to South America with his wife, to evangelise and share the gospel there for many years. Now I had a deep desire for my own further and deeper encounter with the Lord. Stories like that whet one's spiritual appetite.

A lot of these old Christian men have so many golden nuggets and pearls of wisdom one can learn from. Fairly recently I attended a conference with some lovely young Christian ministers, we all had a lot to say on various subjects and our thoughts on them. There was a very old preacher who sat and listened, for the most part. He offered his views on very little unless directly asked. When he did speak, however, those few words tallied up and weighed more often than the many words that preceded them. My advice is for you to find yourself such a person and glean and assimilate all you can. Day after day and night after night I would walk and pray and cry out just to know more of the Lord. That He would visit me and reveal Himself to me in a way I had not previously known.

It grieved me that He had not come to me like that, and yet the old man's story kept resonating with me. The desire for more of God had not waned. Moses felt that too. Amid all the miracles and wonders he cried out:

> *"And he said, I beseech thee, shew me thy glory. And he said, I will make all my goodness pass before thee, and I will proclaim the name of the LORD before thee; and will be gracious to whom I will be gracious, and will shew mercy on whom I will shew mercy."* (Exodus 33v18-19)

He just wanted a deeper encounter with God, and God in His mercy came to him.

It was late on a Friday evening and I had just driven back from Swansea. My children were already asleep and I chatted with Danielle before we went to bed for the evening. In my weariness, my last short prayer was, "Please come tonight Lord, for I cannot live without more of you." At around midnight I woke from a deep sleep, the presence of God filled that room. He had come, and I was so aware of it that I covered my head with my hands and would not so much as open my eyes. My first thought was my smallness and His greatness. Secondly, I felt His presence so real I thought He had come to take me. That subsided, and I realised He had come to bless! I did not want to wake Danielle but I was aware I was physically shaking as God's Holy Spirit was working in me and revealing God's nature and character to me. Bible verses flooded my mind and came alive to me in a way I had never experienced before. I opened my eyes and looked at the clock – it was 4 a.m.

When I turned around Danielle was also aware of His beautiful presence and was silently praying. We got down on our knees by the side of that bed and rededicated our lives to His service. No music, no altar call, nothing of man. Yet a very real and powerful encounter with the Living God. I picked up my Bible and read this Scripture in Amos 7:1: *"Thus hath the Lord GOD shewed unto me; and, behold, he formed grasshoppers in the beginning of the shooting up of the latter growth; and, lo, it was the latter growth after the king's mowings."*

Years before in Whitewell, I remembered the Scripture from Psalm 72:6. *"He shall come down like rain upon the mown grass: as showers that water the earth."* The Bible tells us that all flesh is grass. Just as promised, God's Holy Spirit had come upon me and now for *"the latter growth."*

I love to study church history, theology and various aspects of ministry and shall continue to do so. Yet as vital and beneficial as that is, none of that makes up for a personal encounter with God. In an instant, you see yourself for who you are and see Him in some way for who He is. The Pharisees in Jesus day were great students yet for all that they were cold, blind and hypocritical with no true revelation of who Christ was. John Wesley, the great revival preacher and founder of The Methodists (1703-1791) once famously said: "Catch on fire and the people will come from miles to see you burn."

Isaiah had that very experience in chapter 6v5. *"Then said I, Woe is me! for I am undone; because I am a man of unclean lips, and I dwell in the midst of a people of unclean lips: for mine eyes have seen the King, the LORD of hosts.*" He knew himself and other men (unclean and undone), now he knew God (the King, Lord of hosts). Now his duty was to introduce men to God. Just a few verses later God says "*whom shall I send?*" Interesting God does not mention Isaiah in particular. Isaiah says, "*here am I, send me*" Why? He knows man's heart, and that of the sovereign God, he is now qualified. It is not a degree nor a title, it is a revelation of God.

Dr Colin Hurt (left) and Rev. Yang Tuck Yoong on my graduation 26th May 2016

The Spring of 2016 was such an energetic time, full of hustle and bustle! I was finishing my studies down in Wales and the graduation took place on the evening of Thursday 26th May. It was a well put together ceremony with a personal touch to it as well. Pastor Yang called each student up on stage, shook their hands and presented our certificates alongside Dr Colin. It was an honour to be sure. We lined up and those in ministry came alongside and prayed with each one of us. After that individual and class photos were taken as well as with family members and friends. I look back with fond memories and cherish my time there.

As I previously said BCW had history, and some great teachers such as Duncan Campbell had been there in former times. In my time people like R. T. Kendal and the son of Leonard Ravenhill (David) to name but two had been there. One famous ex-student was Reinhardt Bonke the world-famous evangelist who just passed away recently. Pastor Yang told us he called Reinhardt Bonke, whom he was friends with, and told him he was reopening the Bible College again in Swansea. His reply was "Is it still raining?" Swansea had at the time been voted Britain's wettest city. I can confirm that it is still raining!

Danielle, Molly and Murdo flew down for the occasion and my mum was in attendance too. I was the only person from Scotland from that batch, with friends from the USA, Africa, India, Singapore and many other different nations. It is very comforting to know there is a group of people out there who are part of those filling the great commission of Christ: "*Go ye therefore, and teach all nations, baptizing them in the name of the Father, and of the Son, and of the Holy Ghost: Teaching them to observe all things whatsoever I have commanded you: and, lo, I am with you alway, even unto the end of the world. Amen*" (Matthew 28v19-20).

For my part, Scotland would be my harvest field and where better to begin than my home town of Kilmarnock. Where before I added to the mayhem, now I had the privilege to be an ambassador for Christ. Unfortunately, my friend David had been diagnosed with a terminal illness. Though he could not be there I could never have achieved what I have today without his invaluable input into my life. I remember one day he called me and asked me to visit him in hospital. We spoke about many things and I read a passage from Isaiah:

> "*Why sayest thou, O Jacob, and speakest, O Israel, My way is hid from the LORD, and my judgment is passed over from my God? Hast thou not known? hast thou not heard, that the everlasting God, the LORD, the Creator of the ends of the earth, fainteth not, neither is weary? there is no searching of his understanding. He giveth power to the faint; and to them that have no might he increaseth strength. Even the youths shall faint and be weary, and the young*

men shall utterly fall: But they that wait upon the LORD shall renew their strength; they shall mount up with wings as eagles; they shall run, and not be weary; and they shall walk, and not faint." (40v27-31).

He smiled and said that was his favourite passage. I did not know that. I asked him how he felt about death and he said he had peace about it. I could see on his face that that was true and was the case. I prayed with him and left never to see him again in this world yet with a sure hope of meeting again in that heavenly city where we are promised there will be no more tears nor sorrow. No more death, as it has been conquered, and where we shall know God even as He knows us. What a celebration to look forward to! What a joy! It's real, you know. The question is: Will you be there? Are you sure? How can you get in?

Only one door of entrance. Jesus said: "*I am the door: by me if any man enter in, he shall be saved, and shall go in and out, and find pasture*" (John 10v9).

Pastors gathered at the Kidron House Hotel, Irvine, on Ordination day, 2nd June 2016

In addition, in this whirlwind season, only one week later, on Thursday 2nd June 2016, I was ordained into full-time ministry. Pastor McConnell came over to Scotland and preached at that service in the Grand Hall. Pastor David Purse, who had now taken over as senior Pastor at Whitewell, read from 2 Timothy 4v1-5:

> *"I charge thee therefore before God, and the Lord Jesus Christ, who shall judge the quick and the dead at his appearing and his kingdom; Preach the word; be instant in season, out of season; reprove, rebuke, exhort with all longsuffering and doctrine. For the time will come when they will not endure sound doctrine; but after their own lusts shall they heap to themselves teachers, having itching ears; And they shall turn away their ears from the truth, and shall be turned unto fables. But watch thou in all things, endure afflictions, do the work of an evangelist, make full proof of thy ministry."*

These words ring true to me today and I shall endeavour to fulfil the high calling and privilege of ministry.

It's a strange thing, you know, that I have worked in various sectors in my life and some of these I have been better at than others. Yet all of them felt like things I did – if that makes sense to you? Ministry is not something I do, it is part of who I am. There is no higher honour than to work for God. To be a servant of the Lord. Believe me, there can be tough and even discouraging days, but I would not change it for anything.

Ordination to the ministry
2nd June 2016

To be saved from a lifestyle such as mine is a miracle, to be called into ministry was beyond imagination. "*Now unto him that is able to do exceeding abundantly above all that we ask or think, according to the power that worketh in us, Unto him be glory in the church by Christ Jesus throughout all ages, world without end. Amen*" (Ephesians 3v20-21).

Without a doubt, Christ has done exceedingly abundantly more in the life of John MacInnes. I am delighted my mother was there that evening to see it, just exactly as she had predicted those many years before. It was quite remarkable, quite the occasion.

Eight Whitewell pastors in total prayed over myself and Danielle that evening alongside Dr Colin Hurt from BCW. My good friend Charles Kingsman opened in prayer. There were around two hundred well-wishers there to celebrate with us. I had friends from Singapore, a lady from America, chums from my past life and those in ministry too.

Danielle has been the best Pastor's wife I could ever imagine. Sometimes I wonder how I am doing in the role but I have never questioned Danielle's ability to fulfil hers with an excellent spirit.

I was asked to close that service after the ordination. I spoke briefly from the book of Jonah 4v11: "*And should not I spare Nineveh, that great city, wherein are more than six-score thousand persons that cannot discern between their right hand and their left hand; and also much cattle?*" I felt encouraged as I thought of Jonah that with all his weaknesses the Lord still used him. At least I wanted to be used (I thought to myself).

That verse speaks of 120,000 plus people who needed guidance. The number of people in Ayrshire that year was just over 120,000. While I had no confidence in the preacher, I had every confidence in the message to save and God's heart still to move these many years later.

Informal lunch with Pastor McConnell

Chapter 16

THE SIMPLE LIFE

DURING THE NEXT PERIOD of my life story quite a few people either thought I had entirely lost the plot or had gone bankrupt! Neither of those things was accurate, but there is no doubt it may have seemed more than a little strange to anyone looking at our lives from the outside in.

We made conscious decisions to simplify as much as possible whenever and wherever it seemed viable and reasonable to do so. There were numerous things that I would have to reorganise for that to happen. Also, I was aware it would not happen overnight and even at the time of writing this, there are still a few loose ends to complete the process fully. As the Apostle Paul counsels Timothy: "Thou therefore endure hardness, as a good soldier of Jesus Christ. No man that warreth entangleth himself with the affairs of this life; that he may please him who hath chosen him to be a soldier" (2 Timothy 2v3-4). These verses speak of being called into full-time service as a soldier. It is of course drawing analogies to us being called into a spiritual battle, with no time to be caught up in the affairs of this life. The complications of outside business or distractions.

Now let me qualify that by saying there are many great bi-vocational preachers (men who work a secular job to help fund them in ministry). The apostle Paul was a tentmaker and at times went back to that trade as he laboured in the gospel to support himself and his companions. It's biblical and I have no issue with that whatsoever. My situation however was not like that. I had property that was a burden, a business going on in the background and a house with large financial commitments each month. Many of these things were non-essentials and a hindrance to us in ministry.

I wanted to make the best use of my time. Now you can do a lot of good things but the question is, what are the very best things? The apostles had experienced a similar issue when church growth exploded exponentially in the book of Acts. It is particularly dealt with in Acts 6. A group of widows needed daily feeding which of course was a good thing to do. Yet the apostles said this:

> *"Then the twelve called the multitude of the disciples unto them, and said, It is not reason that we should leave the word of God, and serve tables. Wherefore, brethren, look ye out among you seven men of honest report, full of the Holy Ghost and wisdom, whom we may appoint over this business. But we will give ourselves continually to prayer, and to the ministry of the word."* (Acts 6v2-4).

They would put the correct measures in place but their priority must be prayer and the word. How much more I thought this essential for a newly ordained preacher.

We put our farm property on the market and sold it at a substantially reduced price for a quick sale. I used all the funds to pay off anything I viewed to be an unnecessary tie. It was not so important if there was anything left so long as I was getting rid of obligations and gaining time. One of the assets we owned was a small one-bedroom flat which we rented out in Kilmarnock where the church is. (Our previous home had been in a neighbouring town which was just too far away to allow us to get into working in the community the way we wanted to.) We moved into it and all four of us slept in the same room for the best part of a year! The kids had bunk beds and we just simplified and cut back on all our belongings.

We down-sized our cars, our wardrobes and overhauled our budget and outgoings to a great degree. We would afterwards move to a modest home that was more suitable for the family yet much smaller than anything I had previously lived in. No more acres of grass to cut or hedges to maintain. I can now cut my grass in ten minutes as opposed to most of the day! Danielle and I look back on our time in that flat and we both agree we were no less happy there than we were before. It was a very happy season in our lives.

Never too big for a cuddle from mum!

Next, I had premises overseas that I sold in very unusual circumstances too. We flew out to Spain and I was praying about how best to move on that house when a man came and sat next to me in a communal area. He mentioned he was looking to buy a residence in the same block as his parents but was struggling to find availability and the prices were out of his range. It so happened we were in the same block! I told him that if he offered me the quantity I needed to free us up he could have that one. He could not believe it as it was way below its value. Why would you sell it so cheaply, he asked? It is not about the money it is about quality of life and making it simpler, I explained. I had a great opportunity to share my testimony with him. We booked an appointment with lawyers for later that afternoon and he transferred a deposit on the spot. (I think he thought I may back out of it! He kept saying, 'I can't believe you are doing this!') shortly afterwards it was gone. What previously had seemed a good investment prospect was now just a rope around my neck. I wanted to be free for ministry and was delighted for him that he got a bargain, and near his parents. It was a win-win situation.

Jesus spoke about money on a few occasions. Two brothers approached him. One of the company said unto him: "Master, speak to my brother, that he divide the inheritance with me. And he said unto him, Man, who made me a judge or a divider over you" (Luke 12v13-14). Jesus was not a bit interested in getting involved in squabbling over money, or for that matter getting caught up in the middle of a family feud. As a young minister, I shall try and remember that too! There is a lesson in there.

He also spoke to the rich young ruler and told him to give his money to the poor. Sadly, he choked on that and went away sad for we are told he had great possessions. Little Zacchaeus on the other hand gave half his goods away to the poor without even being asked to do so! Question: Are you more like the rich young ruler or Zacchaeus? It's a thought, isn't it? Much good can be done with money, yet the love of it is the root of all evil.

Later in 2018 my friends who were running Kidron – Dilip and Dinesh (two great lads from Nepal) – were getting ready to move on. That location had two buildings. I sold one to a local businessman and he rented the other part with an option to buy soon afterwards. Again, it was a step towards liberating time.

You never know to what degree God will use you. My thought was this though – the more available I am the more I can be used. Though it may not make financial sense to everyone it was a highly emancipating experience. I no longer live in impressive houses, drive fancy cars, wear designer clothes or have a large bank balance. Yet I can honestly say I do not miss them one little bit. That life brought me no happiness and our life now is reaching out for Christ.

I have already previously mentioned finance but I have felt led to touch on it again here. Now, I am not suggesting one should sell up and live in a monastery. That is neither biblical nor practical. I am however urging you to make yourself as available as possible for the Lord's work. His wages are second to none! He is no man's debtor and unlike this world's currency which you cannot take with you, His wages go on into eternity!

Neither am I saying you should not work. We all have responsibilities to meet. As the Apostle Paul wrote to Timothy: "But if any provide not for his own, and specially for those of his own house, he hath denied the faith, and is worse than an infidel" (1 Timothy 5v8).

Seems strange to me that some people work too much and others don't want to work at all! The Christian life is all about balance. Start from here:

> *"Then said Jesus unto his disciples, Verily I say unto you, That a rich man shall hardly enter into the kingdom of heaven And again I say unto you, It is easier for a camel to go through the eye of a needle, than for a rich man to enter into the kingdom of God. When his disciples heard it, they were exceedingly amazed, saying, Who then can be saved? But Jesus beheld them, and said unto them, With men this is impossible; but with God all things are possible."*
> (Matthew 19v23-26).

Huge wealth and the pursuit of it has distracted many a person from focusing on God first in their lives. Jesus warns against an unhealthy relationship with money. If what He says is true, why would I now try and acculturate huge amounts of it? It makes no sense to me, to be honest.

Remember our Prodigal (Luke 15v11-32) – he did not need all the 'stuff' on which he blew his inheritance. No doubt it seemed nice at the time. What he needed was the relationship restored with his father. After that happened, everything else just seemed to slot into its right and proper place.

I speak with many people who tell me they want a change in their lives. Sometimes I say, 'Ok, let's start by changing this or that.' Often the response seems a little comical and a lot delusional. They want change without changing anything! Now, one does not need to be a genius to see that is never going to work. Overhauling things and cutting back in life can be a daunting thought. Ask yourself: 'Do I need multiple properties, three cars, ten jackets or whatever it is in your case?' Ask yourself: 'Could I use my resources better?' Help someone who is in real need?

As a minister, at times I am with those nearing the end of their lives on earth. I have yet to hear a person say they wished they had worked more or earned more. Some would give all they possess for a few more moments of life. Many speak of regrets of family breakdowns or wish they had done things differently. Do not be such a person. Make the changes now, even if it seems radical to others.

There is a very sad story parable that Jesus shares with us in Luke 16 – the rich man and Lazarus. The rich man had all he wanted while he was alive, while Lazarus sat destitute at his gate begging. The rich man, often known as Dives, had no relationship with him while alive. In eternity Lazarus found peace at last, but the rich man lifted up his eyes in torment in hell. He then made what seems a strange but very specific request – that Lazarus would be sent to administer a tiny drop of water to him. Why not a lot of water? Why Lazarus in particular? Whatever the reasons his request was denied. He had no relationship with him in this life and so it was in the after-life as well.

Much worse though is a failure to have a relationship with God through His Son Jesus. There is no remedy for that after death. There is however a very real and free invitation of the gospel right now. Do not be like the selfish rich man. It was not riches that caused his damnation, but his wrong use of them, among other things. Lazarus, on the other hand, seemed to have nothing in this life – yet if you have a relationship with God it turns out you have all you need. Here endeth the lesson!

CHAPTER 17

BOOKS AND A BOUNCER

EDUCATION is an amazing advantage to have in one's life. My folks were self-employed and education was not too highly valued or pursued in our home. My thought before becoming a Christian was why to bother aiming for university spending years to study when you can earn straight away. The truth is I earned a lot more than most that graduated from university anyway without the swotting or the debt. Since becoming a Christian my view on that has radically changed. There is great benefit in studying and it is now something I do pretty much every day of my life to some degree or another.

Now, I always did endeavour to work hard to improve my skills, whether it was learning in martial arts, cooking, a language or acquiring business prowess. Ministry though is something quite different and I often spend a substantial part of my day reading. The main book I read is the Bible. It is of course far more than a study book. It is God-inspired and God-breathed.

It is a mistake to approach it as a study tool only. You must realise every time you pick it up it is not a great book among other great books. It stands alone and nothing else comes close. That said, studying it will improve many areas of your life if there is an application of the things that you learn from it. Now, you may find it difficult to get past some of the archaic language. Take time to delve into its meanings and you will find it to be a treasure-trove of health and wealth for your soul. The author, the Holy Spirit, is present and willing to unlock its great secrets to the hungry soul and genuine seeker.

It is God's book where He reveals Himself. How this world began and how it will end. Where man's problems came from and the remedy for them. His plan of salvation and the end for those who both reject Him and who are saved by His grace.

I read many other types of books as well. Church history by the likes of Augustine, Martyn Luther, John Foxe and their counterparts. Theologians such as John Calvin, Jonathan Edwards, Adam Clarke, Charles Ellicott, R. C. Sproul, and many more. Great preachers of the past such as Charles Spurgeon, George Whitefield, John Wesley, George Müller to name a few. Preachers of the present, such as Pastor McConnell, R. T. Kendal, Alastair Begg are all to my taste. I try and study a little New Testament Greek each week where time permits, though I am in no way an expert or advanced in it. I read autobiographies and biographies of the great missionaries like C. T. Studd, Hudson Taylor, Robert Jermaine Thomas and some lighter devotional reading too. At times I read secular books on various topics like politics and current affairs. It is important to be aware of what is happening in the world to interact with others and pray intelligently about what is taking place.

Generally, I start with the heavier study and switch over as the day goes on. It is not unusual for me to be reading five or six books at once dipping in and out of them besides Bible commentaries and reference journals while preparing for preaching. That is just how I am wired and it may work quite differently for you. One can learn a lot both good and bad. The successes and the errors are there to be observed and learned from by those who have gone before.

I have very recently started a 3-year diploma in Pastoral studies as an online student at The Shepherds Academy in

Belfast. This is an exciting new development from Whitewell Metropolitan Tabernacle and the brainchild of Pastor David Purse. It is a commitment I am delighted to undertake as it will allow me to learn and grow with people I love and respect while at the same time not infringing on our time in practical ministry where we are now. To get the maximum benefit I see myself not as a pastor so much as a student. I want to be open to all the positive teachings and influences I encounter there, to soak up what I can like a sponge, coming out of it more equipped for Gods work and service.

Now, there is no more boring sermon you will ever hear than a 'book preacher.' The type of speaker who lives in the past and has nothing fresh for today. Read's off a paper in the same monotonous voice, dry as dust without lifting his head or engaging with you in any way. A painted flame but with no real warmth or light. He can be very sound yet send you sound asleep! Yet the opposite of that is a person who studies little and is all froth and bubble with little weight or substance. Both extremes are to be avoided. The secret is to learn from the past and make it your own. Good preachers are like Ruth who gleaned a little here and there before it became her own.

Read deeply and read widely. Now, it is essential to say a few things to fence that for safety: if you are a young Christian and have not decided on where you stand on various issues there is a lot that would confuse you out there. Don't get your theology from Google or Facebook! That's why tying in with a good church is imperative, with people who love and know you and can guide you in your journey.

Yet once you mature there is benefit in reading across the spectrum. Don't only read those who agree with you, but allow yourself to be challenged and stretched. If your beliefs are correct and robust, they will stand the test. I also like to listen to both old and modern sermons. I recently listened to some historic sermons by W. P. Nicolson (1876-1962) for example from Northern Ireland – full of wind, fire and force!

There is much good material out there, and again you can seek guidance from your peers and mentors. I like to attend conferences and bible studies throughout the year as time permits too. The great thing about listening to top-class preachers is you can learn much from them. My advice is, don't only listen to one or you may take on their foibles and weaknesses as well their strengths. I regularly listen to preachers from other denominations too, so long as they are sound evangelicals, it is amazing what you can glean.

All true churches are strong and weak in areas whether aware of it or not. Perhaps one church is stronger in evangelism, another shows great love towards newcomers, another excels in preaching and biblical truths, yet another has a heart for working with youth or another has a giving and generous congregation. A good church should try and have elements of all these things and many more besides. It's so easy to write others off because they are not swimming in the same stream as you are right now. I am not promoting false unity or fellowship at any cost. Bishop J. C. Ryle (1816-1900) once wisely said: "Unity and peace are very delightful; but they are bought too dear if they are bought at the expense of Truth."

One of the pitfalls of listening to online preaching is this – you can scroll through the list of titles and pick what you think you need. Perhaps you think you need a sermon, for example, on faith, but you may need one rather on patience. Whereas if you are physically attending a church you have no idea what will be preached. It may not be anything you would have chosen, yet be exactly what you need.

Books and online materials are fantastic resources and I highly recommend them, but don't exchange them with attending a local assembly. There have been many educated preachers of the highest quality (the apostle Paul immediately springs to mind). People like Jonathan Edwards, regarded by many as one the greatest theological minds to be gifted to the Christian Church or Dr Martyn Lloyd Jones. Yet don't despise those without education, for God can still use them. Billy Bray (1794-1868) from a coal mining background was mightily used of the Lord. He once famously said "If they were to put me in a barrel, I would shout glory out through the bunghole! Praise the Lord!" Or John Bunyan (1628-1688), the old tinker of Bedford, who wrote Pilgrim's Progress among many other Christian classics. The scholar and Puritan worthy John Owen (a great man in his own right) was once asked by King Charles 2nd why ever he would go and listen to such an ill-educated man. He replied: "May it please your Majesty if I could possess the tinker's abilities to grip men's hearts, I would gladly give in exchange all my learning."

Though I have never been to university I have been to the university of life. You can use your past skills and experiences for God yet always look to improve. Not knowledge for knowledge's sake or mere intellectual stimulation, but add to your skills to reach out for Christ.

Matthew 25v14-30 speaks about the Lord giving talents to His servants. One received five, the next two, and the last acquired one. The servants who were given five and two doubled theirs. The servant with the one hid his away. This is what he said, and how the master responded:

> *"And I was afraid, and went and hid thy talent in the earth: lo, there thou hast that is thine. His lord answered and said unto him, Thou wicked and slothful servant, thou knewest that I reap where I sowed not, and gather where I have not strawed: Thou oughtest therefore to have put my money to the exchangers, and then at my coming I should have received mine own with usury. Take therefore the talent from him, and give it unto him which hath ten talents. For*

unto every one that hath shall be given, and he shall have abundance: but from him that hath not shall be taken away even that which he hath."

He neither squandered it nor misspent it. He just did not use it! He was called "wicked and slothful." Let's none of us be like him! Those who used their talents received more, and so it shall be with you also dear friend.

Question: Can you reach a certain group from your background that others perhaps may find difficult to connect with? Are you an academic and can mix in educated circles to share the gospel? Do you have a background with children? – It is the perfect opportunity. "But sanctify the Lord God in your hearts: and be ready always to give an answer to every man that asketh you a reason of the hope that is in you with meekness and fear" (1 Peter 3v15).

I would like to share a story of a man who came to church one day. His name was Archie and he was about seventy years of age. He was well known to me in my past life. He had worked the doors in many pubs and nightclubs as a younger man, spending some time in prison for a fairly serious offence and now worked out at a local gym. His background was in martial arts but his health was now failing. He came along one morning as he had promised to do many times. Once he hesitated at the door and said he would listen from outside. Archie was coaxed in and agreed to sit at the back for half of the service. He never did leave. Weeping during that service and staying to the end. He never missed a Sunday after that unless it was due to ill health.

I have had the privilege of preaching to many people over the years but Archie is the only person I ever remember who cried during every single sermon. He would come to me and say: "I am looking to get to God but I have still not found him"; assuring me he was praying and reading a chapter of the Bible every day. That would increase to five chapters a day over the coming months. He would be one of the first there every Sunday and would bring home baking with him which we put in a tin called "Archie's tin." Smiling and saying "I am the last one in but the first one here." One day he came again weeping and told me he had found Christ. He expressed his great surprise saying: "I never thought I would get to God and I never imagined you would be the person to point me to Him." Just a couple of weeks later he took seriously ill and slipped into a coma never to come out of it again. It was my honour to share that story as I took his funeral – a bittersweet moment for me.

So, the bouncer was born from above and in his own words "was the first one" from that congregation of believers to meet the Lord. Archie had never been a God-fearing man, nor a church attender before that. We had a common link from our past and God provided an opportunity to use that and lead him to the Lord. He was searching for reality and found the Saviour.

God can even use the wreckage of your past for His purposes and good in the future. Don't forget it is never too late to change and never too late to be used by God.

Chapter 18

MINISTRY TODAY

YOU MAY BE WONDERING what we are doing at the time of writing this book. Ministry has various aspects to it. A different hat for every hour of the day so to speak.

As I sit here, we are currently in lockdown due to the Covid restrictions here in Scotland. Hopefully, that will become dated to those who may read this in the future – but it is very real to us at this moment causing many difficult ministry considerations and decisions. That has somewhat curtailed many of our activities yet opened doors for others.

John Knox
A preacher to emulate
(With the family at New College, Edinburgh)

I have previously been involved in quite a bit of work with those struggling with addiction within various Christian organisations. It has been something I have enjoyed and learned a lot from. Though we are still engaged to some extent it does also feel like a new season is dawning which is exciting too. You will find in your Christian journey some things you are involved in are for life and others are for a time and seem to naturally lead on to the next chapter of life and of service. Granted it does bring challenges and stretches one at times, yet there is a great opportunity to preach the gospel and sow into broken lives.

We still welcome those in addiction along and want to point them to Christ. Not everyone is in a place to be helped, and we have responsibilities to look after the whole church including the youth and elderly too. It can be a difficult course to navigate and get the balance, yet very worthwhile too. We want everyone to feel loved and welcome, yet realise we are in a church environment where the worship of God and preaching of His word take centre place.

The Holy Spirit is described as dove-like in the Scriptures. These birds are easily put to flight as they are very sensitive to all that is going on around them. We want the Church to be an atmosphere and environment where God's Spirit visits, dwells and stays. We endeavour to encourage young families in their faith and I would love to work more with youngsters going forward and warn them of the pitfalls before hurt and brokenness take a grip. A child who is saved is a whole life for God.

Many of the Lord's Generals have been saved at an early age. The Apostle Paul wrote to one such, Timothy:

> *"But continue thou in the things which thou hast learned and hast been assured of, knowing of whom thou hast learned them; And that from a child thou hast known the holy scriptures, which are able to make thee wise unto salvation through faith which is in Christ Jesus."*
> (2 Timothy 3v14-15).

Here Paul reminds Timothy of the great privilege he has had learning the scriptures from an early age. He also had a godly grandmother and mother too. Teaching a child God's ways is no small thing in His eyes. I doubt Timothy's relatives had any idea how this young child would turn out as a right-hand man to Paul. He is mentioned many times in the Bible with two epistles named after him.

Danielle does a sterling job with Sunday School and it is certainly an area in which the Lord has gifted her. She has a passion and compassion for children and youth and the Lord has blessed her with ability in that area too. She just quietly gets on with what she is doing in a humble, trusting and prayerful way. She notices things I often do not. When a person is struggling or in need of assistance in some area. She has a gentle touch and a caring spirit. We are both also involved with Scripture Union at Danielle's school alongside two other believers from evangelical churches in our locality. It works ever so well and we count it an honour to speak to those youngsters about the love of Jesus.

I remember reading an interesting account of the renowned preacher Dr Martyn Lloyd Jones one time where he gave a children's talk. Though a first-class expositor of the Word and spoken of in the very highest of terms by his children and grandchildren, his wife is said to have asked him not to try and give children's talks again! It was not his area you see! Great man, godly man that he was – there is a lesson in there for us all I believe.

Ask yourself: Am I willing and available? Also ask: Am I being used effectively or is there someone more suited to this area? Sometimes, ill-equipped as you feel, the Lord will use you there. Other times, he already has a person more suitably prepared. Whatever way, He certainly has something for you to do.

I love the attitude of the apostle Paul. He had what I refer to as a 'green-light attitude'. Someone willing and keen to always be about God's work till he was told differently. This is what we read in Acts:

"Now when they had gone throughout Phrygia and the region of Galatia, and were forbidden of the Holy Ghost to preach the word in Asia, after they were come to Mysia, they assayed to go into Bithynia: but the Spirit suffered them not. And they passing by Mysia came down to Troas. And a vision appeared to Paul in the night; There stood a man of Macedonia, and prayed him, saying, Come over into Macedonia, and help us. And after he had seen the vision, immediately we endeavoured to go into Macedonia, assuredly gathering that the Lord had called us for to preach the gospel unto them." (Acts 16v6-10).

He did not have a red-light attitude, that is, stop doing anything till God moves me. I have on occasion met people with that attitude, often years later you can look back and they still seem to be waiting and never really used to great effect. Paul was willing to go to Asia, but the Holy Spirit forbade it. The result was he went to Europe where of course the gospel spread in an unbelievably productive way.

Question: Are you a red-light person? Stop dead and not moving? Or perhaps at the amber guy or gal, unsure just when you will move? Make sure to be a green light person, one who is always abounding in the work of the Lord.

We have recently participated in a lot of online ministry which has been a blessing for us to be involved in. This would involve posting daily scriptures and quotes from some of the giants of the faith from bygone eras as well as regular online preaching and short messages throughout the week in between. We have been blessed to reach many unchurched and I have frequently noticed individuals from my past listening in whom one may feel are not the most likely of candidates to walk through the doors of a church.

Only a short while ago we launched a new online question and answer session. Wrestling with some of the queries people have started to send to us. I did however put this caveat in – no loaded questions (Jesus was asked many by the Pharisees) – no questions pursuing your agenda (lots of people unwittingly do this). Perhaps they have a certain area they want to focus on, it could be many things and some of them are good. The problem is, that it can lead to every discussion and answer being directed towards a pet subject. Finally, no deep theological questions, which we do not have time to properly address in a limited online discussion. Of course, there is a time to examine such matters, but a short time on social media generally generates more difficulties than it answers!

That said, there is still plenty of scope to discuss real-life issues and see what the Bible has to say about them. Though we try and be as practical as possible the answers do rightly and inevitably come from deeply held theological convictions. I certainly don't claim to have all the answers, but do want to apply biblical values to each question posed. Neither do I claim infallibility as the head of the Roman Catholic Church does, for example on matters of faith and morals. We search the scriptures and discuss what we believe them to mean and look for a lifestyle application of them.

There was a group of Greek Christians mentioned in the book of Acts. They were known as the Bereans. In Acts 17 we read this about the Bereans:

> *"And the brethren immediately sent away Paul and Silas by night unto Berea: who coming thither went into the synagogue of the Jews. These were more noble than those in Thessalonica, in that they received the word with all readiness of mind, and searched the scriptures daily, whether those things were so."* (Acts 17v10-11).

They checked out all that was being said to them in the Scriptures. Remember, it was no ordinary preacher or teacher instructing these guys but the apostle Paul. Still, they looked diligently daily and are called noble for doing so. If we follow their lead, we will not go far wrong.

I have in my past caused a lot of damage and misery in the town where I live and it is now such a privilege to be part of the solution instead of being part of the problem. That said, we can only signpost people to Christ. No use solely introducing someone to yourself. You won't be able to change them. Introduce them to Jesus! The miracle worker whose mission statement is "to seek and to save that which was lost."

We endeavour to build a healthy church for people across a broad spectrum of society, including the older generation, singles, couples, ethnic minorities, welcoming the unsaved, feeding the souls of young converts and of course praying for mature believers to encourage, mentor and help in the various aspects of ministry. Possibly I can relate to someone from my background, but perhaps not so easily with another from a very different lifestyle. That is why it is a 'body ministry'. You might be the very person who could sow into the spiritual life of someone and watch the miracle unfold in their family, home and life. Can you? Will you?

The Grand Hall is an excellent base for us and we are so blessed we are still there. By faith, I can see that place filled as a body of believers reaching out on Kingdom business. Do not look at what you see now; look with the eyes of faith! Remember Abraham, Isaac and Jacob? They could have looked at tents, sand and little of the promises of God fulfilled in their lives. Later, though, it all became apparent. As the writer to the Hebrews put it: *"Now faith is the substance of things hoped for, the evidence of things not seen"* (Hebrews 11v1). How is your spiritual eyesight today as you read this book? In that famous chapter, faith proceeded works which proceeded results! Never forget that.

Unexpectedly, as I sit here penning this chapter, I have realised I am rather enjoying writing. I never would have seen that coming! I compose a blog on our church website each month (see www.grandhallchristianfellowship.org). It is very short and the aim is to be topical and relevant. God's Word is of course, yet as a minister of the gospel, I also have to bring it freshly and practically. Consider Jesus' example. When speaking in a farming community, He shared parables of soils and seeds, while among fishermen He spoke of nets and catches. Learn from the Master. What hook will you put on the line today? There is a mighty catch to be had for the wise fisherman who pays attention to Jesus and His methods.

When considering this book, I concur with the famous French author Victor Hugo who wrote classics like The Hunch Back of Notre Dame and Les Misérables. He once said about a work of his: "I don't know whether this novel will be read by everyone, but it is meant for everyone." Those are my sentiments as I sit and write here today, my aim and intention while writing is to touch and challenge all who read – reader, that includes you! A challenge that ultimately will lead to change. I for my part will focus on the depth of what is written and leave the width of where it will go to God. Perhaps I will write another book? Who knows! I think I would enjoy that. One day it may be profitable to put into words some of those topics from our question-and-answer sessions. Hopefully to help people on their journeys with its twists and turns and daily struggles.

There are many challenges, but Jesus gives a peace that the world cannot give or take away. "*The LORD will give strength unto his people; the LORD will bless his people with peace*" (Psalm 29v11). You can never do God's work your way or in your strength. Thankfully, He promises us His strength if you are one of His, the blessing of peace to boot.

Chapter 19
BUTTERFLY MAN

WHERE WE LIVE in Scotland, and throughout the UK, the butterfly is looked upon as a delicate creature of exquisite beauty. A marriage of vibrant colours, with an iridescent glow. They flutter around, not flapping their wings up and down like a bird but floating gracefully on the breeze bringing joy to those who look on. In fact, in most European counties in general that is how they are viewed. Yet as we shall see, that is not exclusively the case throughout the world. I considered the words of this short poem I came across: 'Love is like a butterfly: It goes where it pleases and it pleases wherever it goes' (author unknown).

You may well be familiar with the term "social butterfly" which indicates a person who moves from one social circle to another. I have moved in various circles during my life but am now delighted to be in a much more stable, loving and secure environment than at any time in my past. As Paul wrote to the Ephesian Church:

> *"For this cause I bow my knees unto the Father of our Lord Jesus Christ, Of whom the whole family in heaven and earth is named, That he would grant you, according to the riches of his glory, to be strengthened with might by his Spirit in the inner man; That Christ may dwell in your hearts by faith; that ye, being rooted and grounded in love."*
> (Ephesians 3v14-17).

This passage speaks of bowing the knee to the Heavenly Father. I pray each person reading has now has done just that.

It refers to family and inner strength that only comes from a relationship with God. Christ living in you causes you to be "rooted and grounded in love." No more need to move and flit about when you are fastened to the Rock who is Christ Jesus.

In Scotland as a young lad, I was once a member of the Boys' Brigade which is a Christian youth organisation founded by William Alexander Smith, combining drills and fun activities based on Christian values. Saying that, I remember one unusual game called "beltie." All the boys stood in a circle with their hands behind their backs. One boy would secretly slip a belt into someone's hand and they then chased the child next to them hitting them with it till they ran around the circle back to their original position! We thought it was a lot of fun, but looking back I don't imagine it would be politically correct or at all acceptable these days! It's funny the things you remember as a child! All the other games were a lot more tranquil by comparison.

Their anthem which was learned and regularly sung is called 'Will your anchor hold?'

Will your anchor hold in the storms of life,
When the clouds unfold their wings of strife?
When the strong tides lift and the cables strain,
Will your anchor drift, or firm remain?

We have an anchor that keeps the soul
Steadfast and sure while the billows roll,
Fastened to the Rock which cannot move,
Grounded firm and deep in the Saviour's love.
(Priscilla Jane Owens (1829-1907), 1882)

It is challenging but brings great hope too. Will you be swept away by the storms of life? When trouble comes, will you drift? Or are you secure in Christ today? As the words of another old hymn put it: "On Christ The Solid Rock I stand, all other ground is sinking sand." It sums it up better than I ever could, in a way so poignant and succinct.

Differing greatly from the European view of the butterfly is one I encountered while in South East Asia where the butterfly was regarded as a fickle type of creature. They had a saying in Thailand, 'Butterfly man.' It is a title with negative connotations. It means a man who is never content but always changing things. Often it refers to regularly changing the girls in your life, but can be used in the broader sense too. I would have certainly fallen into that restless and looking-for-more category. 'Butterfly man' could have easily been used to describe my whims and temperament. Today I am delighted to say it can be used in its most positive and sensitive meanings in my life. I have indeed been blessed to survive all those stages leading up to it. From what felt like a somewhat unsteady start to self-induced devastation and destruction. Growing more brash, brazen and unattractive by the day.

I know what it is to be hidden away when it looks and feels like life is over and you feel at the brink of death with no obvious hope or place to fit in anymore. Yet I also know what it is to experience a genuine bona fide miracle in my life at that very same point. To be changed on every level from deep within; to emerge from that whole experience a new creature with a new nature and desires.

> *"Therefore if any man be in Christ, he is a new creature: old things are passed away; behold, all things are become new. And all things are of God, who hath reconciled us to himself by Jesus Christ, and hath given to us the ministry of reconciliation."* (2 Corinthians 5v17-18).

The old has gone, the new has come, and all by the power of God. To be reconciled to God through Jesus and have the very great privilege of sharing that same story with others just as I am endeavouring to do as you read this today. Metamorphosis in the life cycle of a butterfly, or born again, as the New Testament so aptly calls it.

As we draw to our conclusion, I feel led to recall a party I was at in Glasgow many years ago. I went with a person I had only just met and was among people I did not know at all. After a night of hard partying, marijuana was being offered and consumed to bring people down from all the uppers that had been ingested the previous evening. I had used it before, but in that house, they were doing something new to me called 'buckets.' One uses a bong to burn the weed and fill an empty half-cut plastic bottle with the smoke of it and press it down into water, from there a large amount of it is forced into your lungs. Likely, as it was my first experiment with it and on top of the others narcotics in my system, it caused me to trip. Reality and fantasy were merging to a point that I found myself unable to distinguish which was which. I was gripped by paranoia in the strange surroundings I was in. I sat very quietly in a corner saying hardly a word as the hallucinations grew ever more real. I became convinced my life was a book and could vividly see each chapter unfolding with all the hurts, tensions and anxieties. At points, it flew past so fast I could hardly keep up with what was taking place, yet at others, it seemed to pass excruciatingly slowly. The last chapter though was the great unknown. All I was sure of was that it ended very badly as all sorts of different scenarios tormented me, plaguing my mind. It was quite a memorable yet frightening experience. In retrospect, it's ever so strange to recall that experience. Though it is still vividly etched on my mind, it feels like a different lifetime ago.

Why am I sharing such a strange story as we near the end of this book, you may well wonder? Well, here I am today recording my autobiography, recalling the life events in each chapter. It's quite a surreal experience for someone who has never written before. Many issues I had forgotten about resurfaced. Things I imagined had been dealt with decades ago caused me to smart. Often, I smiled, other times a real sense of sadness enveloped me. I believe it has also helped process some events and feelings too.

I am unsure what the next chapter of my life will be, or how it will end. Even the next day! Yet it is exciting living in the good of it and watching it all unfold. I am positive about this – the story ends well! God has written the ending and I know someday I will be with Christ in heaven which is far better. John MacInnes is heaven bound; hallelujah and glory be to God!

As I reflect on my life, I am humbled and grateful to the One who set me free. As I said at the very beginning – it is His story. I am simply the benefactor and recipient of it. I hope I have been able to share with you a flavour of what my life has been up to now. There are many more stories I could have shared. A lot of them are unsuitable to recount in a public platform such as this is, the truth be told. Yet of all the narratives and anecdotes we have considered together regarding my personal life it is not that important if you recall them or not. If next week you cannot remember my name.

However, the story I share of Christ and free salvation is very different. Never forget the story of free grace and salvation at the cross of Jesus. It is the greatest story ever to be told. My name will be forgotten someday. It may take a generation or two even among my own family. But listen to these words from the metrical version of Psalm 72:17-19:

His name for ever shall endure;
last like the sun it shall:
Men shall be blessed in him,
and blessed all nations shall him call.

Now blessèd be the Lord our God,
the God of Israel,
For he alone doth wondrous works,
in glory that excel.

And blessèd be his glorious name
to all eternity:
The whole earth let his glory fill.
Amen, so let it be

We are but creatures of time, a blip in the timeline of history. All our achievements and influence soon passes away. God on the other hand is outside of time. He is the creator and an eternal being. His name goes on when others do not. His power neither waxes nor wanes. One day every knee shall bow and tongue confess that Jesus is Lord. Either with dread or in love.

We have gone through, I hope, a journey together as you have read this book. Like a roller coaster, it has had its ups and downs, its highs and lows, its hills and valleys. If you are in a valley today look up at Christ, bow the knee and confess Him as Lord. If you are on a high right now, remember we are but finite beings and things change quickly. Put your trust in the unchanging God, I exhort and encourage you to look to Jesus and be saved.

Chapter 20

AN INVITATION TO MEET THE MASTER

IN WHAT FEELS LIKE just a few moments we find ourselves at the final chapter of this book. I desire that it is a brand new chapter in the lives of those who are reading it. A fresh and deeper encounter with God that will be your own unique story and personal miracle. My prayer is you will fly high and live in the freedom of Christ today. Yet you may still be in one of those early chaotic and destructive stages we have considered. The great news is for those who find a relationship with Christ it is just part of the journey and a means of making you aware of how crucial your need is for Him.

Can you recall the narrative of our boy the prodigal? He went from pig feed to the fatted calf just as quick as that. He had his regrets and of course, hindsight is a wonderful thing. Yet not because of his mistakes but despite them, he has a blockbuster of a life story that many of us can identify and resonate within our day to day experiences. It was full of drama, twists and turns, high spirits; on other occasions, you would love to shake and warn him. At times you feel his dejection, pain and regret. For all that it ends well, with love and forgiveness.

Here I extend to you a heartfelt invitation to meet the Master. It's more than just a short one-off prayer that you say in a few minutes and forget, using it like some sort of magic formula or insurance policy for heaven. On the contrary, the Master wants all of you. He wants to take up the reins of your life and lead and guide you at every bend or fork on life's journey.

The question is: Are you willing to surrender and trust Him to take full control? Are you willing joyfully to invite and embrace free access into each area? Are you prepared to ask for forgiveness, trusting in His sacrifice on the cross by faith to grant you liberty and cleansing? "Oh, the blood of Jesus, it washes white as snow." I pray you are. You will never regret it! Christ was and is the Master of relationships. He reaches out to you today with nail-pierced hands of love.

I think it is fitting that in our final chapter of this small book we quote from the final chapter of Gods own book:

"I Jesus have sent mine angel to testify unto you these things in the churches. I am the root and the offspring of David, and the bright and morning star. And the Spirit and the bride say, Come. And let him that heareth say, Come. And let him that is athirst come. And whosoever will, let him take the water of life freely." (Revelation 22v16-17).

In the book of Revelation the word "angel" – which means 'messenger' – can also be used to describe ministers in the churches. For example, in the seven churches of Revelation (chapters 2 and 3), there is a message sent to each overseer which he, in turn, shares with others in his circle of influence.

It has been my great honour to share my memoirs with you and particularly this great message. Jesus Christ is the bright and morning star (Revelation 22v16)! He bids you come to Him. Are you thirsty? Will you taste of the new life He so freely offers? If you do you will reap the benefits in this life and in the world to come.

My dearest reader, I sincerely thank you for taking time out to read my story, and I pray it has been of some benefit to you. As others have shared with me, so I have shared with you. I bid you adieu and God bless. May you soar with Christ from this day forward. "If the Son therefore shall make you free, ye shall be free indeed" (John 8v36).

Much love in Christ – Pastor John (Butterfly man)

Grand Hall, Kilmarnock, in which
Grandhall Christian Fellowship meets
info@grandhallfellowship.co.uk

ACKNOWLEDGEMENTS

One can open a can of worms and unintentionally offend when you start to consider people you would like to thank publicly. I realise many have sowed into my life over the years and I am truly humbled and grateful to every one of you. If you are not named in this brief section, it in no way means I am unappreciative or have inadvertently overlooked you. Time is just too short as is this book to include you all but I am blessed, and thankful to each one of you. There are, however, certain individuals who have helped me during writing this book and of my life that I must acknowledge and personally thank.

- *First my lovely wife Danielle* – Thank you for all your love and support over the years. You are a great wife to me and mother to Molly and Murdo. I am ever grateful you are in my life. You work tirelessly in the background and selflessly free up my time which makes all of this possible. Also thank you for proofreading this book and your valued comments on it.

- *To Molly and Murdo* – I am so proud of you and love you both so much. I pray as you grow physically you will also grow in your understanding of God's love and purpose in your lives. Know this, dear ones – dad loves you very much.

- *My mum* has been unwavering in her love towards me over the years and no words really touch the sides or do justice to thank her enough. She kept believing, praying and is still encouraging. Thanks, mum, I would not be where I am today without you.

- I also want to thank *my dad* whom I love and to whom I am so indebted in my life. You were and are in my corner and I am delighted for our ever-strengthening relationship through all life's ups and downs.

- *Pastor James McConnell,* has been a spiritual father to me over the years. Having intentionally sowed into my life in many ways and on multiple occasions. Despite a relentless schedule, he showed warm heartiness and love that went above and beyond. Philippians 1v3-5 expressed my heart toward him: "I thank my God upon every remembrance of you, Always in every prayer of mine for you all making request with joy, For your fellowship in the gospel from the first day until now." I grew to love and respect him so much over the years and am forever in his debt. [Pastor McConnell went to be with the Lord on 17th July 2021. "Blessed are the dead which die in the Lord from henceforth: Yea, saith the Spirit, that they may rest from their labours; and their works do follow them" (Revelation 14v13)].

- *Reverend John Keddie* – I am obliged and beholden to you as you have encouraged me in the writing of this book and been helpful in it in so many different ways. It would not be the publication it is today without your assistance and expertise. It has been a great pleasure to get to know you better throughout the process. I am overwhelmed by your kindness toward me and offer you a heartfelt thank you.

- *Pastor Yang,* Bible College of Wales, staff and students – I thank you for friendship, fellowship and teaching that has helped me mature and equipped me on my spiritual journey, preparing me for ministry. Bless you all.

- *Jim and Alison McClelland* – When I think of you guys the following Scripture springs to mind: Proverbs 17v17 – "A friend loveth at all times, and a brother is born for adversity." In ministry, you are blessed to shepherd

God's people and share with them the love of Christ. It can in certain circumstances be challenging to cultivate and maintain friendships among those with whom you minister. It has been easy to do so in your case. You have shown unwavering loyalty and commitment to both the church and myself personally. For so many years you have been first in setting up and last out. You have a servant's heart and I am blessed to know and call you my friends. I would also like to thank Jim who is a bit of a grammar buff for keeping me right in that area when writing too. Alison went home to be with her Lord and Saviour on 11th October 2021

- *Charles Kingsman and Douglas Roberson* – I could not have two better friends who have encouraged and supported me. You are men of character and prayer. Ecclesiastes 4v12: "And if one prevail against him, two shall withstand him; and a threefold cord is not quickly broken."

- *Kevin Wyllie, KSG Photography* – Many thanks to Kevin (whom I have known since school) for all your help with the photos. Even though you are extremely busy you still took time out to use your skill and experience. It's greatly appreciated.

- *Alison Dick* of The Secret Place Christian Book Shop, Ballyclare, Northern Ireland – It was so kind of you to put to use your God-given talent and creativity to help to design the book cover. Your enthusiasm and attention to detail have been invaluable.

May the Lord richly bless every one of you. I am privileged to have you in my life.

9781649601889
BV - #0118 - 160625 - C20 - 215/143/8 - PB - 9781649601889 - Gloss Lamination